The Dynamics Of Personal Follow-up

The Dynamics Of Personal Follow-up

Gary W. Kuhne

ZONDERVAN
PUBLISHING HOUSE
OF THE ZONDERVAN CORPORATION
GRAND RAPIDS, MICHIGAN 49506

THE DYNAMICS OF PERSONAL FOLLOW-UP
© 1976 by The Zondervan Corporation
Grand Rapids, Michigan

Zondervan Publishing House, 1415 Lake Drive, S.E.,
Grand Rapids, Michigan 49506

Library of Congress Cataloging in Publication Data

Kuhne, Gary W.
    The dynamics of personal follow-up.

    Includes bibliographical references.
      1. Evangelistic work. 2. Christian life–1960-   I. Title.
BV3793.K83   253.7   75-21126
ISBN 0-310-26951-2

All quotations from the Old Testament are from *The Revised Standard
Version* of the Bible, copyright © 1952, 1956, and 1972 by the Division of
Christian Education, National Council of Churches of Christ in the United
States of America. Used by permission.

All scripture quotations taken from the HOLY BIBLE: NEW INTERNA-
TIONAL VERSION (North American Edition) are copyrighted © 1973,
1978, 1984, by The International Bible Society. Used by permission of
Zondervan Bible Publishers.

Printed in the United States of America

88   89   90   91   92   93 / 25   24   23   22   21   20

Contents

79701

Acknowledgments

I would like to acknowledge my indebtedness to those who have played a role in the development of this book, either directly or indirectly. I must first thank Campus Crusade for Christ for the ministry it has had in my life, both as a student and later, as a staff member. Crusade's influence will inevitably color much of what I write. I wish to thank my fellow staff members with Campus and Lay Mobilization and acknowledge their important role in developing this book. Through their provocative and stimulating discussions on the topic of personal follow-up, and their field-testing of the techniques developed, my understanding of personal follow-up has been greatly enhanced and clarified. I would also like to thank the many who helped in the task of typing and proofing the rough draft of this book. Finally, I want to thank my wife, Karen, who has stood by me and aided me throughout my ministry. She has met my needs completely and has been the primary motivating source in my life. Her typing skills are responsible for the development of this manuscript, and her patience and love are responsible for the project's ever being completed.

May the Lord use this book to stimulate, provoke, motivate, and excite you, the reader, to the joy-filled task of personal follow-up ministry, to His glory.

Introduction

*I have no greater joy than to hear
that my children are living according
to the truth* (3 John 4).

In this verse John is discussing how he felt when he saw the growth in Christ of people he personally taught and nurtured in the faith. He implies that he found greater joy in the effective personal follow-up of new Christians than in any other phase of his ministry. The joy he experienced surpassed even the joy of seeing someone saved. Because I am convinced of the truth of this statement, due to my experiences of the past several years, I have felt compelled to write this book. I have found John's experience to be mine in following up new Christians. It is a joy, however, that few Christians today are experiencing. Studies have shown that less than one percent of professing Christians today have ever been involved in the work of personal follow-up. My own observation, gained through my ministry over a number of years, would place the number even lower than this.

I became a Christian at the age of eighteen. In the years following that decision, while a student at Pennsylvania State University, I became involved in Campus Crusade for Christ. Through the training I received from this ministry, I began to share my faith with others. It wasn't long before I began to see fruit as people prayed to receive Christ as their Savior through my witness. At this point in my life I discovered how important follow-up really was. There grew a real burden on my heart as so many who supposedly had committed their lives to Christ seemed to fall away from that commitment. All these people could not be identified as thorny or rocky soil (see the parable of the sower and the seed in Matthew 13). Since I had received little training in helping a new Christian to grow in his spiritual life, I felt that part of the blame for those who fell away rested on me.

As my burden increased, I began an in-depth search for the training I needed. There was little information to be found. About all I could discover were some ideas on how to give a new Christian assurance of his salvation and get him involved in a Bible study. This forced me to begin independently, through trial and error, to develop methods of personal follow-up to enable me to be more effective in this all-important work. I continued this development of methods after college when I entered full-time Christian service as a staff member with Campus Crusade for Christ. The Lord blessed this project and I began to see a greater number of new Christians growing in their faith as a result of my personal follow-up work with them.

Not long after this the Lord began to impress upon me that there were many Christians who had similar frustrations to mine in the area of follow-up. This led me to try to share what I had learned. I sought to mold my methods into a form easily learned and taught to others. This "transferability" has been accomplished while I have served as director of Campus and Lay Mobilization. Campus and Lay Mobilization (CLM) is an interdenominational training ministry founded in the summer of 1971. It ministers in Ohio, Pennsylvania, and New York. My goal with CLM has been to develop training programs for laymen in the areas of evangelism, personal follow-up, discipleship, and counseling. The major emphasis has been developing effective training in the work of personal follow-up. *The Dynamics of Personal Follow-Up* is an outgrowth of this endeavor. What is contained in this book is not merely theory, but practical insights into personal follow-up proven effective in the ministry of CLM. It is my prayer that this book will serve to develop strong, personal follow-up ministries in the lives of Christians everywhere.

1

Follow-up — An Overview

For many of you who read this book, personal follow-up may be a new concept. It is perhaps a work you have heard about — but you have never actively participated in such a ministry. Don't be ashamed of this. Personal follow-up is simply a ministry that has been neglected by Christian leaders. My experience has shown that the vast majority of people with whom I counsel are not personally involved in following up new Christians.

Studies have shown that less than one percent of evangelical church members are involved in personal follow-up.[1] For many years I thought the lack of personal evangelism was one of the greatest problems facing the church. I have not changed my mind as to the seriousness of this problem. But I now believe the lack of effective follow-up being done in the local church today constitutes an even more dangerous problem for the church at large. Perhaps a few examples from my personal experience will show you the reason for my burden in this area.

One of my first exposures to evangelistic outreach began optimistically. A student at Penn State University, I had been a

Christian for nearly two years. While in high school, before becoming a Christian, I had been the president of the youth group in my home church, and now I felt a strong burden for the youth currently in that group. I sought to find a way to make the gospel clear to them. The opportunity presented itself when the youth leader wrote me and requested that I come and lead a weekend retreat. This was a clear answer to prayer, and with the help of several friends, I set about planning the retreat.

The retreat was finally held and God's Spirit moved in a beautiful way. Only one person out of the entire youth group rejected the gospel invitation. I went back to college rejoicing in the Lord. It wasn't long, however, before I began to have serious doubts about the success of the weekend. The youth leader wrote me and told me about problems arising in the group. Several of those who made commitments were no longer attending. As time went on, all but a few apparently forgot their commitments. I felt helpless to do something about the problem. At that time I did not see the significant role personal follow-up could have played in conserving the fruit of the retreat. This experience jolted me into discovering how to conserve the fruit of evangelism.

Another situation impressed on me the need for effective personal follow-up. This was an evangelistic film outreach in which I was involved. My role was to act as the head counselor, guiding the work of volunteers who counseled with those who came forward in response to the invitation given after the film. The training the counselors received was completely evangelistic in nature and no attention was given to helping the new believer grow in his new life in Christ (I admit this to my shame). The response in the week of film showings was remarkable. Nearly one thousand people came forward to seek the answer to their needs and problems. After approximately six months, I felt burdened to see what lasting result was evident from our ministry. Although communication was a limiting factor, it was still clear there was little lasting fruit from that project. I could account for fewer than two dozen out of the thousand inquirers who still were going on in their decision. I am not relating this to criticize film evangelism; in fact I feel it is a very effective way to communicate the gospel. I am attempting to show that unless there is a strong emphasis on personal follow-up of decisions, there will be little lasting fruit to show for our efforts.

How much difference can an effective personal follow-up program make in the conservation of fruit in evangelistic outreach? Let me cite another example. An evangelistic church with whose ministry I am acquainted reveals an interesting insight into the role of follow-up in fruit conservation. Examining the church records over the past ten years revealed that approximately six hundred decisions for Christ were made in that time. These decisions resulted from a variety of programs, i.e., youth retreats, evangelism weeks, evangelistic services, personal evangelism, etc. The profession of faith statistics, taken from an analysis of membership increase over the same time period, numbered less than one hundred. Thus it would seem that only one out of six decisions was actually conserved. Although this figure does not take into account those who were already members when saved or those who went on in the Lord and joined some other body, it is safe to say that accurate information concerning these other people would not significantly alter the conservation figure of one out of six.

The reason I chose this church as an example is that the leadership in this church decided they could no longer be content with such a low conservation rate. A number of their people received training in personal follow-up and determined to use their training with every person who would respond to the invitation in their church. Soon after that they had an evangelistic week at their church and for the first time sought to follow up on all who responded. After six months the fruit conservation rate was five out of six. Personal follow-up indeed made a significant difference.

My experience over the past several years could multiply these examples of the limitations of evangelism without personal follow-up. Well-planned personal follow-up of new believers could, I am convinced, revolutionize the traditional growth rates of local churches. I believe we can no longer explain away those who don't continue to grow in Christ as being "seeds in bad soil" (see the parable of the sower and the seed in

Matthew 13). Undoubtedly some of those who don't continue to grow in the Lord are the products of "bad soil," yet I see no implication in the text to support a fruit conservation rate of one out of six. Personal experience has shown a much higher rate resulting from effective personal follow-up of new believers. I believe the need is so urgent we can no longer be complacent about so few lasting results in evangelism.

DEFINITION OF FOLLOW-UP

Since this is a book about personal follow-up, it would be good at the outset to define clearly the meaning of this phrase. Because I am unfamiliar with the background of every reader, and the meanings he or she applies to terms, it will be necessary for us to establish some common ground in the area of definitions. For the purpose of this book, follow-up is defined as follows:

*Follow-up is the spiritual work
of grounding a new believer in the faith.*

This is a generally accepted definition by most Christians I have consulted. The following verses are an example of the emphasis the Bible places on this work of building new believers in the faith.

We proclaim him, counseling and teaching everyone with all wisdom, so that we may present everyone perfect in Christ. To this end I labor, struggling with all the energy he so powerfully works in me (Col. 1:28,29).

They preached the good news in that city and won a large number of disciples. Then they returned to Lystra, Iconium and Antioch, strengthening the disciples and encouraging them to remain true to the faith (Acts 14:21,22).

In light of the biblical emphasis on follow-up, the serious Christian has no choice but to do it. The only question that requires discussion is how follow-up can be accomplished most effectively. It is to this question that this book is addressed.

An expansion of the basic definition already given is necessary to clarify the content of this term. The spiritual work of grounding a new believer in the faith is going to be the product of both training and teaching. There are certain basic spiritual truths a new Christian must know and apply to become rooted and really begin to grow in Christ. Chapter 4 deals with this topic in considerable detail, so for our purposes here, only a brief summary of these specific truths will be given. The following is a list of five basic areas of spiritual truth involved in an effective follow-up program:

1. Helping the new believer receive assurance of salvation and acceptance with God.

2. Helping the new believer develop a consistent devotional life.

3. Helping the new believer understand the basics of abundant Christian living.

4. Helping the new believer become integrated into the life of a local church.

5. Helping the new believer learn to share his faith with others.

Another helpful explanation of follow-up would be that it is the assuming of a parent-child relationship with a new believer. This is in the spiritual realm, of course. The Bible describes the new believer as a spiritual baby.[2] This description is an accurate one. Love, protection, food, and training are vital spiritual needs that correspond to the physical needs of a baby. As in the physical realm, a new Christian needs a spiritual parent who will watch over him and help provide these necessities during the early stages of his Christian development.

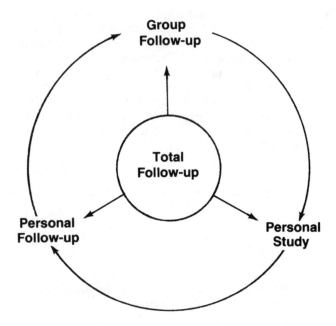

Fig. 1 Elements of a Total Follow-up Program

The work of follow-up in a new Christian's life might be better understood by examining the three basic forms it takes: group follow-up, personal study, and personal follow-up. Group follow-up is that nurturing of the new believer accomplished by the local church or fellowship group. This kind of follow-up takes the form of structured instruction in the basics of doctrine through the use of a new believers' class, or similar program. It also includes the development of committed relationships between the new Christian and the body of believers with whom he associates. The second form, personal study, includes those activities the new Christian engages in on his own. This would include such things as reading books and literature, personal Bible study, and perhaps correspondence courses. On both the group and personal study levels of follow-up there is quite a bit of information available to the average layman to help implement these aspects of a total follow-up ministry. Unfortunately, the same cannot be said for the third form, personal follow-up, which is the major emphasis of this book and can be defined as follows:

> *Personal follow-up* is the assuming of a
> one-to-one relationship by a mature believer
> with a new Christian for the purpose of
> aiding the new Christian's nurture and growth.

This type of follow-up, by far the most effective, as I will seek to show, is the most neglected form among Christians today.

My experience has shown two major causes for failure in personal follow-up. First, many Christians are unclear as to what needs to be done to help ground a new believer in the faith. In some cases, where the Christian has the general knowledge of *what* to say, he is unsure of *how* to say it. This accounts for much ineffectiveness. Secondly, many Christians are unwilling to give the time effective personal follow-up requires. As we will examine later in this book, the time requirements of personal work are considerable. Although there are other reasons for the lack of personal follow-up work by Christians, I will focus upon these two.

IMPORTANCE OF PERSONAL FOLLOW-UP

Having clearly dealt with what follow-up is, the question now before us is: Why is personal follow-up important? That the Bible commands us to follow up new believers has already been shown. But since the work of follow-up takes three forms, I would like to propose four reasons why you should not be content to simply abdicate your personal responsibility in follow-up to the group, or the initiative of the new believer. Rather you should consider personal follow-up a priority on your life and time.

1. The Vulnerability of a New Christian

A new Christian is more easily deceived by Satan than a

more mature Christian. In fact, a new believer is more vulnerable in the fight against Satan's temptations than at any other time of his life. It is common for a new Christian to experience doubt regarding the validity of his decision for Christ. He needs the protection that a more mature believer can help to give him. Victory against Satan's deceptions is only to be found in the truths of God's Word. Christ taught us this by using the Bible to answer Satan's temptations in the wilderness.[3] Knowing little of the Word of God makes a new Christian quite defenseless. This vulnerability is a strong argument for involvement in personal follow-up.

2. The New Christian's Potential for Change

A second important reason for personal follow-up involves the new Christian's rate of growth. A new Christian is at a pivotal point in his life. For the first time, he has the potential for real change in his life style. The direction and guidance offered through personal follow-up greatly increase both the chance and speed of this transformation. Young person or adult, personal follow-up greatly speeds one's growth in Christ. A mature Christian working in such a close relationship with a new Christian is able to detect the areas in his life that need the most urgent change. He is also able to assist in the application of pertinent biblical truth. Without this personal guidance, many new Christians are not able to take full advantage of this crucial period of their lives and do not grow in Christ as rapidly as they could.

A closely related problem is the developing of wrong life patterns in the new Christian who is unsupervised in his growth. These patterns not only hinder his growth, but present unnecessary sin problems that need to be undone in the future before real, lasting growth can take place. This process of change is described in Scripture as a "putting off" of the old man and a "putting on" of the new man.[4] Ephesians 4 and Colossians 3 explain this concept more completely. The truth of these passages should do much to motivate us for the work of personal follow-up.

3. Disciples Are Produced Most Effectively Through Personal Follow-up

A third important reason for doing personal follow-up involves the development of disciples. Personal follow-up greatly increases the speed and probability of discipleship development in a new believer's life. An important and basic goal of your personal ministry in this area is the development of disciples. It is important that the term *disciple* be clearly defined in your mind. My experience has proven that there are almost as many definitions of this term as there are people. For the purpose of this book, a disciple is defined as follows:

> A *disciple* is a Christian who is growing in
> conformity to Christ, is achieving fruit in
> evangelism, and is working in follow-up
> to conserve his fruit.

The importance of developing disciples as part of our ministry is clearly stated in Matthew 28:18-20: "Then Jesus came to them and said, 'All authority in heaven and on earth has been given to me. Therefore go *and make disciples* of all nations, baptizing them in the name of the Father and of the Son and of the Holy Spirit, and teaching them to obey everything I have commanded you. And surely I will be with you always, to the very end of the age.' " An examination of this passage in more depth will uncover an unusual fact. Nowhere is the command directly given to evangelize. Yet, in spite of this fact, this passage is usually given as a challenge for witnessing. Since the main verb of the passage is "to disciple," the core of Christ's command was to go and make disciples. It should be obvious that, implicit in making disciples, it is necessary to first evangelize and win a person to Christ. This must be the first step and explains, justifiably, why this is often looked upon as a passage commanding witnessing. While it is important not to lose this emphasis, we must be careful not to miss the major command. The most important truth of this passage is that of making disciples.

Discipleship training should be a major goal in a total program of personal follow-up. When I use the term *personal follow-up,* I am using it in both a limited and an expanded sense. In the limited sense, I am referring to the initial work of grounding a new believer in the faith. In the expanded sense, I am using the phrase to refer to the entire relationship a mature Christian has with a new Christian over a period of time to help the new Christian achieve maturity. To prevent misunderstanding, I define *discipleship training* as follows:

> *Discipleship training* is the spiritual
> work of developing spiritual maturity and
> spiritual reproductiveness in the life of
> a Christian.

Effective personal follow-up of a new Christian will go far toward conserving more of the fruit of evangelism, but will not in itself speed the fulfillment of the Great Commission. Only an increasing labor force can accomplish this task. The development of spiritual reproductiveness in the new believer's life is the answer to this need. Stated differently, the new Christian must not only be taught to grow in Christ, but he must also be taught to witness and follow up others who respond to Christ. This alone will achieve a truly multiplying effectiveness in fulfilling the Great Commission. This fact brings us to the fourth reason for making the work of personal follow-up a priority in your life.

4. Personal Follow-up Is the Most Effective Way of Achieving Spiritual Multiplication

The degree to which you can encourage a new Christian to be fruit-producing has important implications for the fulfillment of the Great Commission. The previous section showed the truth of this statement. Your effectiveness in this work will determine whether you will be a spiritual "adder" or "multiplier." Will you only *lead people to Christ,* or will you also be responsible for *their leading others to Christ* (these who in turn will lead others to Christ)? Not only spiritual productiveness, but also spiritual reproductiveness should be the focus of your personal follow-up ministry. To be a multiplier should be the goal of every Christian. A multiplier may be defined as follows:

> A *multiplier* is a disciple who is training
> his spiritual children to reproduce themselves.

In other words, a multiplier is a disciple who is able to produce other disciples. Only when this process occurs will we see true spiritual multiplication. I define multiplication as follows:

> *Multiplication* is third-
> generation discipleship training.

To further explain, third-generation discipleship training is seeing someone you have personally discipled discipling another to disciple others. It is extremely important to understand the concept of spiritual multiplication, for it is the goal of this book to produce spiritually multiplying Christians.

Spiritual multiplication is a process that goes through four distinct phases. An explanation of these phases aids in the understanding of this concept.

Key
WITNESSING =

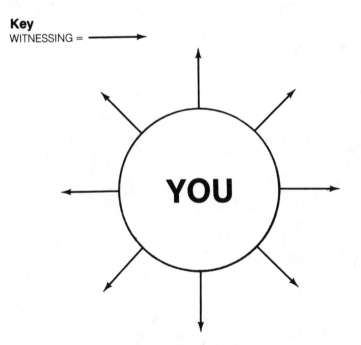

Fig. 2   Multiplication: Phase One

Phase 1: Evangelizing. The first phase in spiritual multiplication occurs when we share our faith with other people. As was already explained, the command to witness was implied in the Great Commission command of Matthew 28:18-20. There can be no short-cut. It is essential that you share Christ with others. Although the *method* of evangelism may vary widely, the *message* cannot. As you share Christ in the power of the Holy Spirit, you will begin to see results, i.e., fruit. When an individual repents and receives Christ as his Savior and Lord, you begin a second phase of the multiplication process.

Key

WITNESSING =
FOLLOW-UP =

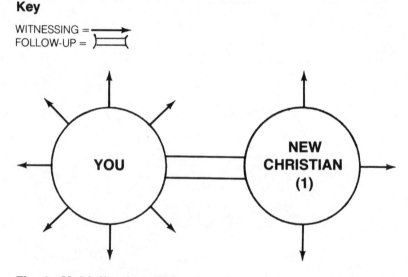

Fig. 3   Multiplication: Phase Two

Phase 2: Personal Follow-up. Phase 2 of the multiplication process occurs when you personally start to follow up a new Christian. You begin to meet with him on a regular basis to give him the basic care and teaching he needs to grow in Christ. While in phase 1 all your ministry time was spent in witnessing, now in phase 2 you are beginning to devote a growing percentage of your time to the work of building the new Christian. You continue to share Christ even while you are involved in the work of personal follow-up. It is important not to neglect this work. Part of your work in follow-up involves challenging the new believer to a public identification with Christ and a proclaiming of the gospel, i.e., witnessing. When the new believer begins to do this you have, in effect, doubled your evangelistic outreach as the result of working with another believer to get him involved in witnessing.

It is important to remember that witnessing by itself does not go far enough to fulfill the Great Commission. At a certain point in time, either when a new Christian has grown sufficiently in Christ or when he leads someone else to Christ, a new phase must begin. You must start to train the new Christian to personally follow up someone else (ground them in the faith). This is what has been previously defined as discipleship training, or "discipling," for short. When you begin this distinct phase of personal ministry, you begin phase 3 of the multiplication process.

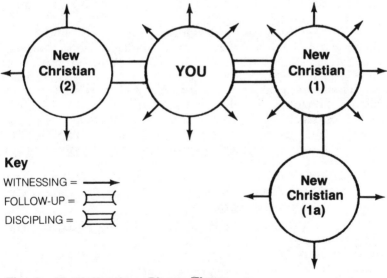

Fig. 4 Multiplication: Phase Three

The Dynamics of Personal Follow-up

Phase 3: Discipling. Phase 3 begins when you start to train the Christian you are working with to personally follow up another new Christian. This is a distinct phase because now you are working with a new Christian to enable him not only to keep growing in Christ, but also to become effective in the work of personal follow-up. This not only adds people to the witnessing team, but it also adds them to the fruit conservation team. Phase 3 is obviously a longer phase than phase 2 because it takes much longer to train a new Christian to do personal follow-up than to help him begin to grow in Christ. The work of phase 3 goes through three distinct levels:

1. Teaching him to follow up someone.
2. Teaching him to teach others to follow up someone.
3. Teaching him to teach others to teach others to follow up someone.

The goal is the multiplication of teachers. This is the truth Paul sought to relate to Timothy in 2 Timothy 2:2: "And the things you have heard me say in the presence of many witnesses (level 1) entrust to reliable men (level 2) who will also be qualified to teach others (level 3)."

Examine this phase more closely and you will find a great increase in the number of evangelistic contacts. This increase is the product of multiplication of laborers, not the product of increased witnessing on your part. An even more significant point that comes out if you examine phase 3: There are now more people to do follow-up. Now you are multiplying your effectiveness in outreach. It is also important to notice that as you go into discipleship training with someone, you will probably see more fruit and be forced to start follow-up all over again with someone else.

You probably have a question at this point: Why is there another phase for multiplication? Multiplication really begins when two factors are present:

1. A person has been discipled through level 3 (2 Tim. 2:2).
2. A person actually begins to take someone else through a discipling process.

Thus, multiplication must go beyond merely training and teaching, the goal of phase 3, to implementation. And this brings us to phase 4.

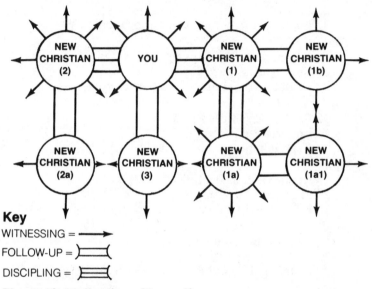

Key

WITNESSING = ➤

FOLLOW-UP = 〉▭〈

DISCIPLING = 〉▭〈

Fig. 5 Multiplication: Phase Four

Phase 4: Multiplying. Phase 4 is the multiplying stage of the multiplication process. This is where 2 Timothy 2:2 has become a reality in your ministry. Phase 4 occurs when a person, followed-up and discipled by you, is following up and discipling others. This is the goal of your follow-up ministry and can be accomplished no other way than through one-to-one involvement and training. The fulfillment of the Great Commission is a reality only when 2 Timothy 2:2 becomes a reality. We must evangelize, follow up, train, and send if we are to see the world evangelized. If you only develop one truly multiplying disciple each year (not an unreasonable goal), examine what growth will take place for the gospel outreach as a product of your life over a six-year period. Assume that one evangelistic contact per week is made by each disciple:

Year One
    1. Begin year: 1 disciple (you)
    2. End year: 2 disciples (you, plus 1)
    3. Evangelistic contacts: 50 approximately

Year Two
    1. Begin year: 2 disciples
    2. End year: 4 disciples
    3. Evangelistic contacts: 100 approximately

Year Three
    1. Begin year: 4 disciples
    2. End year: 8 disciples
    3. Evangelistic contacts: 200 approximately

Year Four
    1. Begin year: 8 disciples
    2. End year: 16 disciples
    3. Evangelistic contacts: 400 approximately

Year Five
    1. Begin year: 16 disciples
    2. End year: 32 disciples
    3. Evangelistic contacts: 800 approximately

Year Six
    1. Begin year: 32 disciples
    2. End year: 64 disciples
    3. Evangelistic contacts: 1,600 approximately

In a six-year period, if you only discipled 6 people, you will have caused the eventual development of 64 disciples and the evangelistic confrontation of 1,600 people per year. This is how the multiplication process works. If you continued the process for ten years, you would have personally discipled 10 people and witnessed to 50 a year — but you will have caused the development of 1,024 disciples and the annual confrontation with the gospel of approximately 25,000 people. This isn't just mathematical juggling but the logical outgrowth of faithful working for the Lord.

The most important "why" of personal follow-up is answered by a firm grasp of the vision of multiplication. My hope is that enough Christians catch this vision to fulfill the Great Commission. A survey of the rapid expansion in world population growth makes the need for multiplication urgently clear.

FACTORS AFFECTING PERSONAL FOLLOW-UP

Personal follow-up, as I have defined and expanded it, does not occur in a vacuum and is not entirely free of restraints which inhibit its growth. There are a number of factors which control and regulate the effectiveness of your discipling ministry. Some of these factors are quite obvious and scarcely need mentioning; others are perhaps less obvious and would be important for you to consider and ponder. The following is by no means an exhaustive list of conditions governing effective personal follow-up ministry, but it is comprehensive and should, if nothing else, stimulate your own evaluation of barriers facing your ministry.

Factor 1: Relationship

Any study of factors affecting personal follow-up ministry must begin by examining the personal needs of the "discipler." It is important that you be in right relationship with the Lord in your own Christian experience. As will be stressed continually throughout this book, personal follow-up is not only methodology, but also life transference. Thus there can be no substitute for a dynamic relationship with Christ in your own life if you seek to be effective in helping someone else grow. There will inevitably be a loss of effectiveness if you try to bypass this rule. There is a subtle temptation, as you begin to gain insights into methods, to begin to rely on a certain method, or perhaps a sequence of instructions, to achieve an effective personal follow-up ministry. I know from personal experience how this can become a source of real ineffectiveness in personal follow-up. My point in making these comments is not to imply that follow-up training is inappropriate or unnecessary (this book is evidence of my conviction of the necessity of this very thing). I am only attempting to point out at the beginning that any important truth can be taken to an extreme and perverted into an error. Methodology training in follow-up is meant to *supplement*, not substitute for, personal life communication. Paul clearly focuses on the role of life transference in 1 Thessalonians 2:8: "We loved you so much that we were delighted to share with you not only the gospel of God but our lives as well, because you had become so dear to us." A new Christian's growth can be killed in the bud if you focus on methods at the expense of relationship.

Factor 2: Commitment

Multiplication is the product of both personal follow-up and discipleship training and thus is a time-consuming process. Anything that takes time also takes commitment. Perhaps more than any time in history, the average person today is extremely busy. There are many different needs and problems vying for his attention and involvement. The Christian is not immune to these pressures. In fact, the growing Christian perhaps feels them even more acutely because of the time requirements of church involvement which the non-Christian does not face. With the variety of demands on a Christian (i.e., witnessing, worship services, classes, committees, Bible studies, prayer meetings, etc.), a legitimate question is whether or not the time requirements of personal follow-up are valid in light of projected results.

If an individual begins to do some personal follow-up, he is soon faced with a problem of priorities. There is simply not enough time to do everything. He must soon come to a decision on what his priorities are and establish, in the light of his priorities, what are legitimate activities. I hope the previous discussion of the necessity of multiplication has assisted you in perhaps rethinking priorities. Some necessary questions that need to be asked in your own life are:

"Do I believe in the importance of personal follow-up?"

"Am I willing to spend the time necessary to develop disciples?"

"Am I willing to rethink my present involvements

and discontinue those which are no longer a priority?"

Asking questions like these and honestly seeking to answer them will go a long way in causing you to become effective in personal follow-up. Only a committed person is willing to spend the necessary time in follow-up. If you are not totally sold on its importance, as soon as problems and frustrations begin to occur, you will leave to find greener, easier pastures. Commitment plays an important role in the development of effective multiplication.

Factor 3: Concentration

Effective follow-up can never take place if you are attempting to work with too many people at one time. Multiplication depends upon spiritually mature and well-trained disciples. This type of disciple is never mass produced, but rather is the product of in-depth, time-consuming, hard work. To achieve true productiveness, you must work with only a few people at a time. Second Timothy 2:2 makes a point about the type of person on whom you should concentrate: *Faithfulness* is the criterion for concentration in the process of multiplication. It is important that you have faithful, trustworthy individuals who will reproduce themselves in this ministry. If you focus your work on a few people for a period of time and they prove untrustworthy, you will have nothing to show for your work. Chapter 7 elaborates on how to choose faithful disciples.

You will need to be totally committed to the concept of personal follow-up to stand against the pressures you are sure to face. The pressure not to concentrate your energies on a few is going to be great. You will be called selfish and unspiritual, among other things. I remember a pastor who was upset by my insistence on this principle. He told me, "I see that the Bible teaches this idea of concentration, but it is clearly unworkable in the church of today. I have too many responsibilities to concentrate my energies." He was unwilling to adopt the biblical method because it would mean changing his traditional method of ministry. What a tragedy.

It is important that you withstand this pressure. This will be possible only if you have a long-range view of your ministry and are not tyrannized by the urgent needs around you. Robert Coleman, in his perceptive book, *Master Plan of Evangelism*, states that concentration was one of the basic elements of Christ's discipleship methodology.[5] Early in His ministry, Christ chose a core of men and began to pour His life into them. His purpose was to create the leadership necessary to adequately oversee the growth of the early church. In a real sense, Christ staked His entire future effectiveness on these few men. He did not misread God's will in this matter. Under the empowerment of the Holy Spirit, these disciples multiplied, taking the gospel to Jerusalem, Judea, Samaria, and the world (Acts 1:8).

Perhaps the following diagram will be helpful in illustrating the concentration technique employed by Christ. Starting with Christ at the center, the time spent varies inversely with the distance from the center.

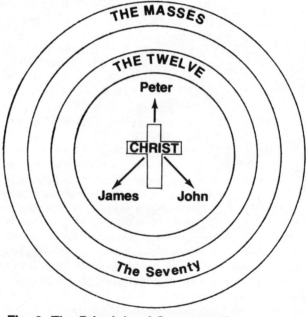

**Fig. 6 The Principle of Concentration
in the Ministry of Christ**

Waylon Moore, in his book, *New Testament Follow-up*, discusses various laws governing multiplication. One of the most important is the factor of concentration. He states: "A decision that our ministry will be intensive, rather than extensive will change our whole life. Quality begets quantity. It takes vision to train one man to reach the mass."[6] There is no substitute for the role of personal discipleship development and this can only occur when we concentrate our energies.

Factor 4: Duration

It is going to be exceedingly important to your personal follow-up ministry that you understand and accept certain time requirements. Follow-up is not only a temporary time drain for you, but it will also continue over a period of time, possibly for a year or more. It is important to realize this, not only because you need to be committed to working that long, but also because it will take time for the results of a multiplying ministry to become obvious to those looking on. If you are unsure about the time requirements of multiplication, you will be left without a defense when people criticize you for spending so much time with so few. The truth of this factor is obvious from the discussion of the rate of growth in multiplication over a six-year period (see previous discussion, pp. 27-28). A look at the ministry of Christ is also a convincing demonstration of the truth of this principle.

Christ poured three years of His life into the twelve apostles. Near the end of this time (approximately six months), He spent nearly all of His time with them. Thus Christ, the master Discipler, felt it necessary to do this to insure the massive multiplication of the Christian church over the following quarter of a century. If there had been a better way, Christ would have used it. You would not have been too impressed if you had been an uninvolved bystander at that period of time. There were not more than five hundred followers at the time of Christ's death and many of these were only peripherally involved. Yet Christ was satisfied with His work, for He saw in His disciples the future multiplication of the church.

Waylon Moore stresses this principle and its application to the encouragement of discipleship. He states that it takes multiplication approximately three to five years to become obvious.[7]

This means it takes that long before people become aware of the growth becoming obvious in their midst. Many laymen and pastors are afflicted with a spiritual short-sightedness. They do not seem to notice the groundwork laid for a ministry program over a period of years, but rather they see only what you are currently doing to achieve growth. This explains why so many have missed the truth of multiplication for so long.

Perhaps more than any other person, the late Dawson Trotman, founder of the Navigators, has contributed to the development of a multiplication vision in the church today. His booklet *Born to Reproduce* relates his personal experience in follow-up. In this book he shares his frustrations at seeing "decisions" that did not become "disciples" in his ministry. He also relates the length of time he spent with a man and the long-term multiplication it produced, to prevent the previous frustration from continuing.[8] I pray that you will gain the vision necessary to insure the duration of ministry required for follow-up and multiplication. Remember Isaiah 60:22: "The least one shall become a clan, and the smallest one a mighty nation; I am the Lord; in its time I will hasten it."

Factor 5: Teaching and Training

Personal follow-up is by definition a product of teaching, training, and spiritual growth. The first elements in follow-up imply that, to a certain extent, the growth of a new believer will be the product of the training of the person doing the discipleship. Thus, the availability of training in the area of personal follow-up is an important part of multiplication. If you have understood our discussion of multiplication, you can readily see its importance.

If personal follow-up is to become effective and produce multipliers, an individual needs the training to initiate the process. One of the reasons for a book such as this is the regrettable lack of training available for the average layman. This book will certainly not meet the need entirely, but it is a step in a positive direction. If it causes a few people to begin to do personal follow-up, practical experience can become an effective substitute teacher.

Not only is it important for the one doing the discipling to receive adequate training, but it is also important that he give the new disciple adequate training to work with someone else. Without training the new disciple to work with others, you will never get beyond second-generation discipling (see discussion on pp. 24-28 on third-generation discipling). As obvious as this truth seems on the surface, I have found that practically no one grasps it. Perhaps the problem lies in the lack of transferability in most training. By transferability I mean the ease by which a training program can be taught by a learner to someone else. If your method of personal follow-up is haphazard and learned primarily through trial and error, it will be hard to train someone else to follow up another the same way. This is why I have spent several years trying to develop transferable insights into personal follow-up ministry. This book is part of the product of that effort.

There is another element in the role of teaching as it affects personal follow-up. The new believer needs to become involved in a church with expositional teaching. By expositional teaching I mean the teaching of the Word of God by showing doctrinal implications and life applications, with insights from the original languages. A new believer needs more than exhortative sermons for growth. He needs a strong input of the Word of God as meat, not milk. Doctrine is much more effectively communicated on a group level by teaching than on a personal level by sharing. Waylon Moore makes a convincing argument for the role of the teaching ministry in the development of disciples.[9] It is a factor which cannot be overlooked.

Factor 6: Environment

The final item to be analyzed in our discussion of factors controlling the effectiveness of personal follow-up ministry is the role of environment. This is the spiritual environment the new believer encounters, not his physical environment. The kind of spiritual environment a new believer experiences will play a large part in his subsequent Christian growth, or lack of it. It definitely makes a difference where a new Christian has fellowship. The spiritual temperature of the church in which a new believer finds himself will control to a certain extent the vitality of his life. A lukewarm or cold church environment can be devastating to a new Christian's growth.

A cold or lukewarm environment in a local church strikes at the credibility of what you are teaching the new Christian. In personal follow-up you are talking about the joy of life in Christ, the love of the brethren, the need to witness, the role of Bible study, the fruit of the Spirit, etc. When a person attends a church where these qualities are not evident, he begins to doubt whether you are really being honest with him. A person generally conforms to the characteristics of his environment. A new Christian will conform more readily to carnal Christian living than to spiritual Christian living if that is the prevalent spiritual climate. Perhaps this explains why Christ was so strong in His denunciation of the church at Laodicea in Revelation 3:14-22. Christ says in verses 15 and 16: "I know your deeds, that you are neither cold nor hot. I wish you were either one or the other! So, because you are lukewarm — neither hot nor cold — I am about to spit you out of my mouth." I had always looked at that verse in light of how lukewarmness strikes at the credibility of evangelism, but more recently I have discovered its effect on follow-up as well.

Where are you sending your new Christians? Are you creating the right spiritual environment for their growth? It is important in personal follow-up to insure that a new Christian is exposed repeatedly to a vital, vibrant Christian fellowship. If you cannot feel safe in bringing a new Christian to your church, how will you answer him convincingly when he asks you why you are still going there? Environment not only plays a role in a new Christian's growth, but also in the growth of more mature Christian's as well.

CONCLUSION

Multiplication is indeed the only solution that holds promise for the fulfillment of the Great Commission. It is important to become involved in the personal follow-up of new Christians with a view toward multiplication. You must not only ground a new believer in his faith, but also take the further step of training and developing him to become effective in working with others. When you do this, you will begin to set off a chain reaction in multiplication.

There are certain factors which act to control the effectiveness of your personal follow-up, and you need to be aware of them and be able to deal with them. For example, your relationship with Christ will control your effectiveness, so you need to be consistently growing in the Lord. Follow-up is in a real sense transference of life, not just information. It will take genuine commitment to the work of follow-up to give it the necessary priority in your life.

You cannot mass-produce disciples, but rather you must concentrate your energies on a few. It is, therefore, very important to pick out faithful men who will reproduce your life in others. It will take time not only to develop disciples, but also to begin to see obvious growth from the multiplication process. This needs to be understood to prevent discouragement.

The role of training must not be understated in any discussion of personal follow-up. Primarily one does what he is trained to do. You must train a new Christian to work with others. It is also important that he receives strong biblical teaching. Finally, because environment will play a strong role in effective follow-up, do everything possible to get a new Christian involved in a warm, growing church.

Why not pray and ask God to enable you to work with faithful disciples and multiply your life in others? Remember 2 Timothy 2:2: "And the things you have heard me say in the presence of many witnesses entrust to reliable men who will also be qualified to teach others."

The Dynamics of Personal Follow-up

Notes

[1] Waylon Moore, *New Testament Follow-up* (Grand Rapids: Eerdmans, 1963), p.19.

[2] John 3:3; 1 Corinthians 3:1; 1 Peter 2:2; 1 John 2:12-14

[3] Matthew 4:1-11; Luke 4:1-13; Mark 1:12,13

[4] For an excellent discussion on the dynamics of change in a Christian's life, read: Jay Adams, *Competent to Counsel* (Grand Rapids: Baker, 1970).

[5] Robert Coleman, *Master Plan of Evangelism* (Old Tappan, NJ: Revell, 1963), pp.21-37.

[6] Moore, *New Testament Follow-up*, p.68.

[7] Ibid., p. 69.

[8] Dawson Trotman, *Born to Reproduce* (Colorado Springs: Navigators, 1974).

[9] Moore, *New Testament Follow-up*, pp.40-41.

2

Follow-up
Begins With You

It should be apparent from the previous chapter that any meaningful discussion of personal follow-up must begin by examining the person doing the follow-up, for it begins at home base. For your personal follow-up to be effective, certain characteristics must be true of you. As we examined in the previous chapter, personal follow-up is much more than merely imparting information — it is the imparting of your very life. This is clearly seen in Paul's attitude as expressed in 1 Thessalonians 2:8: "We loved you so much that we delighted to share with you not only the gospel of God but our lives as well . . . ."

Thus it is important to begin this discussion with an examination of the prerequisite factors involved in developing the ability to transfer your life to another person. This chapter may be an uncomfortable and perhaps convicting one to read, because it will show that we are sometimes lacking in actions or attitudes necessary for real effectiveness in personal follow-up. The following is a discussion of a number of factors that must be characteristic of a Christian's life if he is going to see effective personal follow-up taking place.

Factor 1: **Be Open and Involved**

This first factor concerns your openness and vulnerability to people. You must allow yourself to become involved with another person. Often we don't allow ourselves to become involved beyond a certain point because it is so threatening and time-consuming. Think about your life for a moment. To be open and involved with someone is a conscious decision you have to make. This will be an important decision. It is possible for you to go through the motions of personal follow-up but never be truly open and vulnerable to people. While your follow-up won't be very effective, you could still sit down and mechanically go through the motions. It is possible to minister in a detached way *to* people and never become involved *with* them.

Early in my Christian ministry I approached people in just this impersonal way. My role was purely that of dispensing information. I remember one person who requested we stop meeting because he had as much information as he could use. His problem was knowing how to apply what he already knew. I felt bad about no longer meeting with him, yet it never occurred to me to go beyond my formal role in follow-up and become really involved in helping him learn to apply the truths I was teaching. I had the feeling I ought to do something, but I was so unsure of my own application of biblical truth that I opted for the safer route of noninvolvement. It wasn't long, however, before I could no longer live with my noninvolvement and detachment. It turned out to be too late for the Christian with whom I was working. That sad experience motivated me never again to allow myself to work in a detached way with people.

One step toward developing this attitude in personal follow-up (and indeed it is an attitude that needs developing) involves learning to view a new Christian from God's perspective. In 2 Corinthians 5:16 we are told we must no longer view men from a human point of view. Once a person becomes a new creation in Christ we must forget our human perspective and view him the way God does. A practical example of this changed perspective is seen in the way Christ viewed His disciples. Obviously, after He began to work with them, especially in the initial stages, it must have been discouraging from a human standpoint. They were constantly failing their Lord. In the face of their failures, Christ needed to view them in the light of their potential as new creations in Him. I'm certain this is also the way God looks at us. Since Christ viewed His disciples as God the Father viewed them, even in the face of failure, He was motivated to continue to develop them to their true potential.

In personal follow-up, you are in somewhat the same situation. As you begin to work with a new Christian, it will be a subtle temptation at times to become discouraged with his progress. You might begin to feel you are wasting your time. Some of these new Christians might not seem to have much potential in and of themselves. Yet it will be important to continue to view them as God views them. God can use and develop anyone into an effective instrument for His work. If you can gain this vision, then you will be motivated to do what is necessary to insure that the new Christian with whom you are working becomes productive in the outreach of the kingdom. One way to insure this is by working closely with him and allowing yourself to become involved. He must know you are there, that you really care, and are available and open to him.

By emphasizing the need to be available and open to people, I am not implying that you are merely to be a sounding board for people's problems. I also am not implying you should allow people to leech on you and your time. Rather, your role in personal follow-up is to be confronting people with their problems and helping them to solve them.

Another step in developing this attitude in personal follow-up is a willingness on your part to be honest with a new Christian. Don't put up a front. What often happens in personal follow-up is that a counselor goes into a follow-up situation and pretends he is a spiritual giant or that he has all the answers. When this happens, it creates a false front and prevents honesty with the new Christian. Sometimes we are afraid to admit we have had or are still having some problems in our own lives because we think it will hurt our credibility. This fear is groundless in follow-up.

Be human and don't seek to appear perfect to the new Christian — unless of course you are! In that case you have gone past the point Paul reached near the end of his life when he wrote the Book of Philippians. In Philippians 3:12 he writes: "Not that I have already obtained all this, or have already been made perfect, but I press on to take hold of that for which Christ Jesus took hold of me." Perhaps you are past this point in maturity Paul had attained. That's possible but not probable. If you are not, don't try to appear perfect and with discretion share some of your own defeats in the past. Then share the biblical solutions you have found. This will be very helpful for the new Christian's growth. If you haven't found any solutions, you need to get working. If all you can share with the new Christian is defeat, you will not be much help to him.

Factor 2: Believe in the Importance of Personal Follow-up

Do you really believe the personal follow-up of new believers is important? Your answer to this question will determine in a large measure your effectiveness. As I will be repeating again and again throughout this book, personal follow-up will only be done by those who are willing to spend the time it requires. Since there are time demands, involvement in personal follow-up obviously comes down to a question of priorities. Who, or what, will take the highest priority positions in your life? Personal follow-up will not be a priority until you become burdened with the need for it. Unless this ministry becomes a priority, you will never do it. Let me emphasize also that endurance in the face of problems is only possible if follow-up is a high priority for you. If you are not convinced of the necessity of personal follow-up, you will not have enough motivation to deal with the problems without quitting. For these two reasons it is important to settle the question of priorities when it comes to personal follow-up ministry.

Factor 3: Desire to Be Used

The desire to be used of God is a vital attitude to have in your life. Can you honestly say before God that you desire for Him to use you? Remember, when God begins to use you, it usually means much hard, but satisfying, work. Consider carefully before you answer this question.

A look at Scripture will point up the importance of this

attitude in your life. A good example of this is found in Isaiah's vision of the Lord related in Isaiah 6. After seeing how utterly sinful he was before God, Isaiah was in the right frame of mind to respond honestly to God's call on his life. We need to look at ourselves and others as God views us before we can be adequately motivated to desire to be used by Him. The Lord finished the vision to Isaiah by giving him a challenge. Examine closely Isaiah's response: "And I heard the voice of the Lord saying, 'Whom shall I send, and who will go for us?' Then I said, 'Here am I! Send me' " (Isa. 6:8). There was no doubt as to Isaiah's sincere desire to be used — and God honored that desire and used him.

Another example of this factor is seen in Paul's attitude in his letter to the church at Rome. Follow what he says in this passage:

> I long to see you so that I may impart to you some spiritual gift to make you strong. . . . I do not want you to be unaware, brothers, that I planned many times to come to you . . . in order that I might have a harvest among you. . . . That is why I am so eager to preach the gospel also to you who are at Rome (Rom. 1:11-15, italics mine).

There is little doubt here as to Paul's priorities and desires. You will find the need and importance of desire expressed in the Lord's teachings contained in the Sermon on the Mount: "Blessed are those who hunger and thirst (real desire) for righteousness, for they will be filled" (Matt. 5:6).

The question at this point is a practical one. How can one demonstrate his desire to be used? Is it simply a matter of telling the Lord of the desire? The Bible makes it clear this is not enough. James 1:22 tells us we are to be doers, not merely hearers of the Word. Actions must support each verbal commitment. There are a number of things one may do to demonstrate his desire to be used. He could obtain as much training as possible in the area of evangelism and personal follow-up. This is a practical way to demonstrate one's desire. The better equipped one becomes, the more effective an instrument he is in the Lord's hands. It would also be helpful to be consistent in outreach. This enables one to be where the action is when it comes to personal follow-up. It is clearly unprofitable merely to talk without taking action in the communication of a desire to be used by God.

Factor 4: Being Available

Closely aligned with the importance of desire is the need to be available. Availability is a tremendously important principle in Christian service. God can use anyone, in spite of his limitations, as long as he is available for His use. Conversely, no matter how skilled and effective one is, if he is unavailable God cannot use him. The Bible abounds with examples of this truth, and I shall discuss two of them.

First, look at the call of Jeremiah found in the first chapter of the Book of Jeremiah. Here the role of availability becomes obvious. After the Lord called him, Jeremiah began to find many excuses why he couldn't do what God desired him to do. These excuses took the form of some of the more common alibis you find even today. Jeremiah complained that he was too young, untrained, and not much of a speaker. These were really unworthy excuses and merely a cover for his lack of availability. The Lord showed that He could override any of Jeremiah's limitations and only desired his faithful obedience. When this became clear, Jeremiah became available for God to use.

Perhaps the best biblical example of availability is the story of God's call on Moses' life at the burning bush. This is the best display of excuses and responses I can find in Scripture. Moses' encounter with the burning bush is told in Exodus 3:7-10. There God gives His first call to Moses. This begins a two-chapter verbal struggle between God and an unavailable Moses.

Moses' first excuse is found in Exodus 3:11 —

> But Moses said to God, "Who am I that I should go to Pharaoh, and bring the sons of Israel out of Egypt?"

His excuse was that he was just an average person and not cut out for the Lord's service. Even from a human standpoint this was a faulty argument, since Moses was raised in Pharaoh's courts and was infinitely better equipped to do the job than anyone else. But for those who feel this kind of an argument is sufficient to prevent them from doing the Lord's will in personal follow-up, look closely at the Lord's answer:

"But I will be with you" (Exod. 3:12).

When you are a Christian you are never simply a "normal nobody." God is with you and that makes you somebody. Thus this excuse is a weak one, yet it is still frequently used today.

Moses' next excuse involved the problem of authority. He felt he couldn't be God's instrument because he had no authority. I have found this a common problem in follow-up today. There are many Christians who feel they have no authority to challenge people to become Christians and live for Christ. They feel they have no authority to direct the path of another person in personal follow-up. Look at God's answer to this excuse:

And he said, "Say this to the people of Israel, 'I AM has sent me to you' " (Exod. 3:14).

This is God's answer to you. You *have* the authority to do personal follow-up and direct the path of a new believer because God gave it to you. When you use His Word and are empowered by His Holy Spirit, you are under His authority when you minister!

Next Moses tried the old credibility excuse. He thought his work would be ineffective because no one would believe him. He felt he had nothing to show to answer their unbelief. Moses stated the problem this way:

Then Moses answered, "But behold, they will not believe me or listen to my voice, for they will say, 'The LORD did not appear to you' " (Exod. 4:1).

I have heard this (imagined) problem of credibility expressed over and over again. But this was no problem for God. He gave Moses the rod which became a serpent, and He also backed up his witness with the plagues. You are probably thinking that if God would do such things for you, you wouldn't have this excuse either. But the truth is, God has done even more for you. The greatest miracle of all is a changed life. There is no earthly explanation for the miracle of conversion. You do have all the credibility you need for a personal follow-up ministry.

Moses had still more excuses. His next centered on his natural limitations. He and Jeremiah match up on this point:

> But Moses said to the LORD, "Oh, my Lord, I am not eloquent, either heretofore or since thou hast spoken to thy servant; but I am slow of speech and of tongue" (Exod. 4:10).

This would seem to be a good excuse if it weren't for the Lord's answer:

> "Who has made man's mouth? Who makes him dumb, or deaf, or seeing, or blind? Is it not I, the LORD? Now therefore go, and I will be with your mouth and teach you what you shall speak" (Exod. 4:11,12).

As in Jeremiah's case, natural limitations are not a problem for God; instead, they serve to reveal God's power all the more.

Moses had one excuse left. It was his last and best. God has no answer for it. Moses was unavailable:

> "Oh, my Lord, send, I pray, some other person" (Exod. 4:13).

Since Moses made himself unavailable for God to use, the Lord was forced to use Aaron as the mouthpiece in the delivery of His people. The obvious application of this is that you simply must be available. Lack of availability is the only limitation preventing your effectiveness in follow-up.

Availability is of prime importance for effectiveness in follow-up. My own experience has shown that God can use anyone if he will only become obedient to Him. Professors, corporate executives, skilled technicians, and common laborers have been effectively used by God when they determined to do His will. I know of an individual crippled with arthritis who is confined to a wheelchair, whose follow-up ministry has been responsible for many people now in full-time Christian service. Would that we could learn to trust God totally to work through us in spite of our limitations.

To say that availability is important is not to downplay the role of training. Certainly training will improve your effectiveness, but the best training in the world will accomplish nothing unless one is willing to be available for God to use. Are you available?

Factor 5: Consistency of Life

The next factor concerns life style. Perhaps nowhere else is the need for consistency of life more evident than in the work of personal follow-up. As you begin to spend the time required to do an effective job of personal follow-up with a new Christian, it will become increasingly difficult to hide an inconsistent walk with the Lord. You can fool someone for a time, but the truth will inevitably come out. There can be no substitute for a consistent example in personal follow-up.

Why is consistency so important? Because demonstration plays such a large role in developing people. The most powerful influence a parent has with a child is in the area of demonstration. A child will remember and follow a parent's life far more than his teachings, especially when the two are at odds. I remember a powerful commercial on television a couple of years ago connected with the campaign to get people to stop smoking. A father and son were walking together and everything the father did, the son copied. This even extended to smoking. The reason for this commercial's power was its basic insight into the truth of demonstration. Like will beget like and there is no way to prevent this from happening. You *will* reproduce yourself. The only real question revolves around *what* you will reproduce, not *that* you will reproduce. You will either lead or mislead — there is no middle ground.

This explains the emphasis on consistency in Paul's writings and the importance he placed on both his own example and the example of others:

> Command and teach these things. Don't let anyone look down on you because you are young, but set an *example* for the believers in speech, in life, in love, in faith and in purity (1 Tim. 4:11,12).
>
> We did this, not because we do not have the right to such help, but in order to make ourselves a model for you to follow (2 Thess. 3:9).
>
> Brethren, join in imitating me . . . (Phil. 3:17 RSV).
>
> Follow my example, as I follow the example of Christ (1 Cor. 11:1).

Not only is the positive aspect of example taught in the Bible, but there are also warnings against the power of example to mislead. A key argument Paul used in combating problems in the church at Corinth was to warn of the danger of leading others into sin through example. Much of Paul's emphasis about the danger of false teaching in the pastoral Epistles grew out of the ability such teaching had to be spread by demonstration. In 2 Timothy 2:17, Paul uses the word "gangrene" to describe the effect of bad example. How much more descriptive a word can be used to describe the effect of the example of bad teaching?

While consistency of life style should be our goal as Christians whether we are involved in personal follow-up or not, the work of personal follow-up often gives us the added motivation we need to be consistent. If you really believe you will reproduce yourself, that like begets like, then you will be more apt to live consistently. Christ taught the truth of like begetting like in Luke 6:40. There He described the dynamic of discipleship as a reproduction of the discipler in the disciples: "A disciple is not above his teacher, but every one when he is fully taught *will be like his teacher*" (RSV).

There is no middle ground for you as a discipler of men. You must be a good example or you will, by default, be a bad example. The motivational power of example will be explored more extensively in chapter 6. Remember James's warning in James 3:1 and prepare well for the work of follow-up: "Not many of you should act as teachers, my brothers, because you know that we who teach will be judged more strictly" (James 3:1).

Factor 6: Growing in Christ

It is extremely important that in the midst of a personal follow-up ministry, you continue to grow in your own relationship to Christ. You must never assume you have arrived. You must keep striving to grow in Christ more and more. The believer will reproduce only what has been developed in his own life. He will never bring anyone past the point he has reached in his personal growth in Christ. Remember Luke 6:40 on the dynamics of discipleship: The disciple will only be like his teacher. Naturally it is possible that someone else could help the person you are following up to grow beyond your level. But you can never cause the person to grow beyond your own level of maturity. This truth certainly must be conditioned by the fact that after a certain point in growth, subsequent growth is not so much a product of nurture. Rather, it is the result of personal surrender and obedience. Admitting this does not really make your need of personal growth any less valid since you can also prove to be a hindrance to someone's growth if you are not growing.

Paul left us a good attitude to adopt in seeking to understand God's will regarding growth. Even in the later stages of his life, when he was writing the Book of Philippians, Paul expressed his attitude toward his personal need for growth in the following way:

> Not that I have already obtained all this, or have already been made perfect, but I *press on* to take hold of that for which Christ Jesus took hold of me. Brothers, I do not consider myself yet to have taken hold of it. But one thing I do: Forgetting what is behind and *straining* toward what is ahead, I *press on* toward the goal to win the prize for which God has called me heavenward in Christ Jesus" (Phil. 3:12-14).

To sum up Paul's position, he pressed on and strained forward to grow even more in Christ. Is this your attitude? In Philippians 3:15, Paul states that those who are really mature in Christ are like-minded. What does this tell you about your stage of spiritual maturity? Don't stagnate, but continue your own growth in Christ. Your effectiveness and fruit in the Lord's service will be in direct proportion to your yieldedness and maturity.

Factor 7: Accepting Yourself

A person's attitude toward himself has a marked effect upon his follow-up effectiveness. One who has not come to a personal self-acceptance will be limited in his ability to work effectively with other people. If you have never been able to accept yourself, you will unconsciously be afraid others won't accept you either. This unconsious fear tends to prevent you from being open and honest with people. As we mentioned earlier, this openness and honesty is extremely important in personal follow-up. The fear causes us to build false fronts in our lives that make us appear more acceptable to others. When this happens, the transparency of life, so important to effective relationships with other people, is destroyed.

This lack of self-acceptance that I am discussing involves our unwillingness to accept ourselves as God created us. This means we have never accepted our physical appearance and abilities (or lack of them), our mental limitations, and the unchangeable aspects of our environment, both economic and physical. We rebel against the parents God gave us and the economic position in which we find ourselves growing up. These attitudes and others show our resentment toward God for giving us a "raw deal." We are bitter and have never really come clean before God. It would be impossible for us to voice Paul's attitude expressed in the following verses:

> And we know that in all things God works for the good of those who love him, who have been called according to his purpose (Rom. 8:28).
>
> . . . I have learned to be content whatever the circumstances (Phil. 4:11).
>
> Give thanks in all circumstances . . . (1 Thess. 5:18).

Until we get right with the Lord and accept ourselves as He made us, believing He had a perfect plan in making us the way He did, we will never be really effective in follow-up.

When I speak about accepting yourself, I am not implying that you should overlook the sin in your life. You should never be content with sinful problems. God desires you to deal with them and gain the victory. Maybe you were born with freckles and red hair, but you weren't born with a temper. You developed it sinfully over time. Perhaps you were born into a rich family, but you were not born lazy. Laziness was the product of sin in your life. Can you see the distinction? God never wants you to accept sin, but He does want you to trust Him and His wisdom in the midst of unchangeable circumstances. It is important to deal with this sin problem in your own life and in the lives of the people you are following up. To be effective in working with other people, you must have really accepted yourself.

Conclusion

My purpose in this chapter has not been to deal with all the factors involved in your growth in Christ. Indeed, to do this would take an entire book, maybe several. I have only sought to comment on those attitudes and actions which have direct bearing on the work of follow-up. I am firmly convinced that personal follow-up is more the communication of a life than it is the communication of information. To be open and honest with a new believer is basic to developing a relationship with him. Strong belief in the importance of follow-up is vital if one is to give it the proper priority. Desiring to be used is a necessary attitude in insuring more than just talk when it comes to follow-up. Availability is important because this is the only problem in follow-up for which the Lord has no answer. Being a consistent example is essential because of the powerful role of demonstration in follow-up. Continuing to grow in Christ is required because you cannot bring someone beyond the point you have reached in your own spiritual growth. Acceptance of self is basic to being open and honest with the people you follow up.

I trust that this list of attitudes and actions which affect follow-up have stimulated your thinking and motivated you to prepare for effective follow-up.

3

Developing a Meaningful Relationship With a New Believer

Developing a close friendship with a new believer is a basic ingredient in effectively following up a new Christian, for it involves a nurturing that goes beyond merely the teaching and enforcing of rules. It also involves a loving communication of those rules and a loving communication of a life.

Early in my Christian ministry, I had a difficult time developing relationships with new Christians. The problem was my approach. I was assuming that relationships just naturally occur. In some cases they might, especially if the individual has some areas of interest in common with you. Unfortunately, in personal follow-up you will often be working with someone with whom you have little in common. In this circumstance, it will take concerted effort to build an effective relationship. Over time I discovered a variety of "tools" for building relationships. Along with these came a thrilling sense of spiritual victory in my own life. No longer was I limited to certain types of people for effectiveness in my ministry. I have found a similar joyous response in people I have trained in follow-up ministry. In Christ there is truly neither slave nor free, Jew nor Greek.

Spiritual parenthood has many of the same characteristics as physical parenthood. How many of us could be content merely to be a rule giver and enforcer with our children? In addition to being an authority figure, a good parent is constantly seeking to know his children better and develop a meaningful relationship with them. This is also true when it comes to effectively following up a new Christian. We do need to be authority figures, i.e., spiritual leaders who communicate the how-to's of growing in Christ. At the same time, however, we must also be developing meaningful relationships with new Christians. The purpose of this chapter is to offer some practical advice on developing this relationship with a new Christian.

Develop an Atmosphere of Loving Concern

A friend loves at all times, and a brother is born for adversity (Prov. 17:17).

One of the first ways to begin developing a meaningful relationship with a new Christian is by being honestly concerned for him, really wanting to be his friend. Paul clearly teaches this as one of the important elements in his own follow-up ministry. For example, examine the way Paul described his attitude toward the Philippians in Philippians 1:8: "God can testify how I long for all of you with the affection of Christ Jesus." He begins by saying, "God can testify." It is important to understand why he starts this way. Paul doesn't use this term lightly, but rather uses it only when he wants to make something unquestionably clear to us. When he said, "God can testify," Paul knew he was calling an omniscient God to witness to the truth of his statement. This was necessary because of what Paul went on to claim about the way he felt toward them: "God can testify how I long for all of you with the affection of Christ Jesus." What a statement! This describes the point I am trying to make. How much do you really care about the people you are following up? Do you love them with the affection of Christ? If you do, then the relationship is bound to develop; if you don't, the relationship will be hindered. We need to build into our lives the attitude in which we can say with Paul, "God is my witness" (RSV), I'm burdened over that new Christian.

While I was still a student, I remember working with a young married student. Although I worked hard, I seemed to be getting nowhere in my follow-up. I was unable to gain his confidence and our relationship was a shallow one. One day while thinking about the problem, it occurred to me that I really didn't care about the fellow. I wasn't burdened for his growth, but rather was slightly irritated at the trouble he was causing me. What a sobering and convicting discovery this was! I determined to begin to focus my prayers and concern on him as a person, and to seek to develop the love God desired me to have for him as an individual. It wasn't long before there were some real breakthroughs in follow-up. That young man is now serving God effectively in full-time Christian service.

Do you genuinely want to help the new Christian grow in Christ? Do you honestly care about people? If you feel you need more love and concern to answer in the affirmative, you can pray and specifically ask God to develop that kind of attitude in your life. Through prayer God will give you this type of burden. The Bible doesn't explain why the mechanics of prayer work this way, but there is something about interceding for a person that increases your burden for him.

Pray for specific things. If you run out of things to pray for, start reading the first part of many of Paul's Epistles. There he makes specific prayers for spiritual growth on the part of the new believers. In your prayers insert the name of the person you are following up. If over a period of time you keep praying for him in a disciplined way, God will develop that burden within your heart. You probably won't notice it grow, yet soon you will find yourself sincerely caring for that individual.

There is one exciting implication of this truth I want to emphasize. You can feel a burden for, and thus build a relationship with, someone you would not naturally choose for a friend. When I was in college I had a pastor who helped me a great deal in my own Christian growth and thinking. Once he said something I will never forget: "Before you became a Christian *you* picked out your friends. After you became a Christian, God began to pick out your friends and often He picks out people you never would." When you are forced into relationships with

Christians whom you would never choose to be your friends, it *forces* you to turn to God for the strength and love you need to develop the relationships. In personal follow-up you can't pick and choose who is going to respond to Christ. Sooner or later you are going to find yourself in personal follow-up relationships with people you would not normally choose to spend time with. God can work around that problem. He can give you the attitude you need to develop a friendship with those people.

When seeking to build friendships with new Christians it is important to have an accepting kind of love. Jesus applied this principle of accepting love as He worked with His disciples. His love and concern for those disciples were basic tools in their spiritual growth. They knew He loved them and there was never any doubt in their minds. Even when they failed the atmosphere was one of concerned acceptance. The Lord rebuked them when they failed, but He still loved them and continued to work with them, helping them to learn from their mistakes. In spite of their failures, they knew Christ's love was unconditional.

An important question to ponder is whether you are creating or will create this kind of environment or atmosphere of unconditional acceptance and love for a person. Please don't misunderstand. This doesn't imply overlooking their sinfulness, but rather, it means accepting them in the face of their failings and showing them how to deal with any problems they have. You can love them and help them discover God's way out of it. It is possible to accept the person and at the same time not accept the sinful shortcomings in his life. As you work with people, do you create that kind of accepting atmosphere?

A good way to test yourself is to check out why the new Christian does what you assign him. Is it the result of his motivation to grow in Christ — or is he afraid that if he slips up, you will reject him? Is he performing for your sake, or the Lord's? When pleasing you is the exclusive motivation in a new believer's life, there is something seriously wrong. It's going to be extremely difficult to develop in that person the proper kind of motivation. Are you creating the kind of an atmosphere of love which is helping to motivate the new Christian to grow?

Develop Your Relationship Around Christ

A second major truth in building relationships is to develop your relationship around Christ. It is important to realize that this will take real effort, because the natural thing is to try to develop a relationship around something else. You develop a relationship with one person because he likes basketball, with another because he likes art. Having things in common is a good aid in developing a relationship, but when it becomes the center or focus of your relationship, you become limited in your circle of friends. In 1 John 1:3 John gives us the correct focus for lasting relationships: "We proclaim to you what we have seen and heard so that you also may have fellowship with us. And our fellowship is with the Father and with his Son, Jesus Christ."

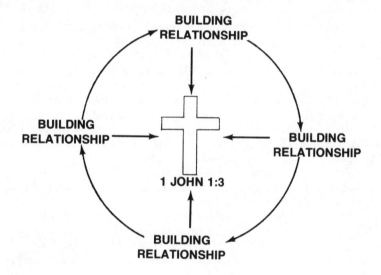

Fig. 7 Focusing Relationships on Christ

John gives Christ as the focal point of true fellowship. He claims that relationships should be developed around knowing Christ. This does not mean it is wrong to have other things in common with a person you are following up. What it does mean is that often you are going to be put in a follow-up relationship with someone with whom you have little in common. This should not prevent you from having a meaningful relationship and friendship if Christ is at the center.

How do you make Christ the focus? From the very beginning of follow-up with a new Christian, spend the bulk of your time on spiritual things. This doesn't mean lecturing that person, but it does mean devoting most of your time to spiritual communication, creating an atmosphere of spiritual sharing. Make it a natural thing to share with one another what God is doing and what God is teaching you through His Word. This develops naturally only when it is the way you act in the initial stages of that relationship. If you develop your relationship around something else, you will have to force Christ-centered discussion, and it becomes an awkward, unnatural thing. If you develop your relationship from the beginning around Christ and spiritual things, the pattern is set for future openness.

There is another important factor in developing your relationship around Christ. Whenever you are with a new Christian, strive, formally or informally, to share something spiritual. Since formal sharing and teaching occurs naturally when you meet to go over a follow-up appointment, there is no need to elaborate on the formal aspect of this truth. But let me give you a few examples of what I mean by informal sharing:

One tool you might use to develop a relationship with a new Christian is a common interest in baseball. I am talking in terms of youth work here, but the application will be obvious for those working with all age groups. Going to a ball game is a secular activity used for developing relationships. Even in the midst of a game you can be teaching, however. I know one person who has thus shared one of the ways God made a distinct change in his life in the area of attitudes. When he played baseball in school he was aggressively involved in the game. This attitude carried over when he became a spectator. His aggressiveness would express itself beyond yelling and cheering. He also verbally assaulted various referees he didn't think were doing a good job. His attitude was sinful. But God changed him and gave him victory over the problem. By sharing this with the new Christian, he was able to show in a practical way how God makes a difference in the Christian's life. This is a good example of communicating a spiritual truth informally. It may not have been an ideal teaching environment, yet informally he was communicating a deep spiritual truth to that new Christian.

Another example of this informal teaching might involve two women who go shopping together as a tool for developing their relationship. Perhaps there are many people around, and it is hectic. This is a perfect opportunity to share how you used to get frustrated and uptight in this kind of situation, but God has given you patience and peace to keep a good witness for Him in the face of adverse circumstances (Phil. 4:10-13). If God hasn't done that work in you yet, it will be impossible to share in this way and you shouldn't lie about it. However, this example should make the point clear to you that even in secular situations, you can have an informal time of sharing. You ought to be communicating something positive continually.

As a student at Penn State I made it a rule never to meet with someone for follow-up or discipleship unless I had something fresh to give him. I wanted to share something new God had taught me or reinforced in my mind during my personal study of the Word. As God has given me strength, I have never since that time failed to communicate a fresh spiritual truth when I met someone for follow-up. You don't have to keep reaching back into your memory. If you are in the Word, the Lord gives you something constructive every time. It might not be a brand-new insight, but it can be a reinforcement of a truth you already knew. And you can always communicate this kind of truth. This is the best way to get the new Christian to the point where he will begin to share with you, too.

A question at this point might be how to motivate people to study the Word. Although I will deal with this in detail later, a preview might be helpful. The best way to motivate a new Christian toward Bible study is to use the Bible when you deal with his problems and share how you use it when you are solving your own problems. Jesus motivated His followers to use the Word mainly because He used it. In answer to their questions and problems Jesus quoted the Old Testament 160 times in the presence of His disciples. And that is how you motivate men to use the Word.

Stick-to-it-ness

The next important factor in developing relationships with new believers involves the ingredient of stick-to-it-ness, or patience. It takes time to build relationships. You will not develop a lasting, meaningful relationship with a new Christian in three follow-up appointments. In your first few meetings you can lay the groundwork for a good relationship and set the basic preconditions for it to occur; but the relationship itself will not develop that soon.

The reason for this is obvious. How long does it take you naturally to develop a close relationship with someone? The spiritual realm is no different. The new Christian's relationship with God is going to take time to develop, and it is also going to take time for that new Christian's relationship with you to grow. Friendships will not always grow smoothly, or even at the same rate. Sometimes a new Christian might not seem to be responding at all, yet you need to stick with him.

The fact that a person isn't growing at a certain rate or always being victorious over sin should not discourage you. A person may stumble one week and the next week be renewed from the Word, getting back on the right track once more. Although discouraging, these periods of defeat are not disastrous for one's overall Christian life. This is especially true if one learns from his failures. Learn to have patience in the face of failures. Everyone falls down once in a while and the new Christian you are following up is no exception.

Do not take it personally when the new Christian stumbles. This is a problem I find often arises among those doing personal follow-up. In other words, you will sometimes be tempted to take the new Christian's stumbling as a reflection on your follow-up expertise. How dare he fail after you did such a good job communicating how not to fail? Of course, sometimes we need to become upset. This motivates us to help our young Christian friend deal with his problems. But when we become upset because our feelings are hurt and our pride is trampled upon, then we are sinning. Our main concern should be that the sin is hurting the new Christian's growth.

Patience is also required to discern the new Christian's attitude in the midst of the failure. Is he repentant, wanting to learn from his mistake, or is he rebellious? It is important that you have discernment at this point. Attitudes at times are not clearly reflected by actions. This is true because actions, in many cases, are controlled by both the past and the present environments in which the person lives. It takes patience and discernment to discover the inner attitude of the new Christian. But you *can* find it because God reveals it to you. It is difficult to detect attitude problems if you don't really know what is happening inside an individual. Although you won't totally understand a person's problems and attitudes, you do have the leading of the Spirit to give you a sensitivity others lack.

In his encounter with Ananias and Sapphira in Acts 5, Peter gives us a perfect example of this sensitivity. He was able to see beneath the surface of the problem by detecting wrong attitudes. This example also shows there may be sinful attitudes present even in the right kind of actions. Only in Christ is it possible to gain this type of insight.

Another important element of stick-to-it-ness is being willing to reprove the new Christian when he needs reproof. Whenever he stumbles, it is important that he deal with his problem. In other words, confront him with his sin and then show him how to solve the problem and get back into a right relationship with God. The idea here is to use both the corrective and rebuking aspects of the Word of God as they are revealed in 2 Timothy 3:16,17. More will be said on this point in chapter 5. Stick-to-it-ness is essential in personal follow-up.

Spend Quality Time Together

> There are friends who pretend to be friends, but there is a friend who sticks closer than a brother (Prov. 18:24).

The next factor to consider in developing relationships is the role of association. By association I mean spending time with the new Christian. In youth work it is somewhat easier for the association to take place than with adult work, since an adult's time is much more rigidly structured by family responsibilities and similar restrictions. Yet, in spite of the difficulty involved in finding time to spend with an adult who is a new believer, it is still necessary that we do so. For instance, housewives might meet over mid-morning coffee, those in business over lunch. Choose an optimal time for both of you.

When seeking to find activities that aid association, look for something you are already doing to which you could invite the new Christian. This is the key to finding time to do effective personal follow-up. By doing two things at once, you squeeze forty-eight hours into twenty-four. It is possible to piggy-back your time to aid you in association.

One example of how to accomplish this would be to take the new Christian with you when you go to church. The reason you take him with you is not simply to get him to go to church, although that is one reason. It is also for that twenty minutes driving home when you can discuss the sermon. The important thing is just spending time talking together and fellowshiping. Not everything I do for association is feasible for everyone, but we can each find some way to spend time with a new Christian. It might take some effort, but the real problem is one of burden, not time.

Robert Coleman in his book, *Master Plan of Evangelism*, has a good discussion of the role of personal association when it comes to effective follow-up.[1] He states that spending time with the new believer is the essence of a truly effective follow-up program. I tend to agree with him on this point. The following is a list of examples of activities that are easily piggy-backed with association. I hope it will stimulate your own thinking.

1. Going to church	6. Camping
2. Attending church activities	7. Picnics
3. Shopping	8. Holiday activities
4. Going to sporting events	9. Short trips
5. Washing your car	10. Etc.

A new Christian often becomes most open and honest about his victories, defeats, problems, etc., in the informal times. Do all you can to create these all-important times of informal fellowship with a new believer.

Be Interested in More Than Just His Spiritual Life

The next factor conditioning the development of effective relationships with new Christians concerns the problem of viewing our role from too limited a perspective. We can sometimes become overly concerned about the spiritual side of a person's life and neglect other aspects involved. Each individual is made up of many parts which form a single whole with all of the parts interrelated. The spiritual affects the social and the social can also affect the spiritual. This interrelatedness is found in every area of a person's life, and because of this you have to deal with more than the spiritual needs of a new Christian.

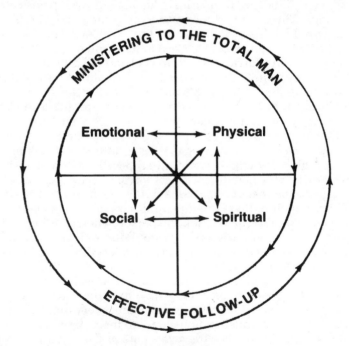

Fig. 8   Following Up the Total Man

For example, let's consider the possible relationship between a social problem and a spiritual need in a new believer. An important aspect of personal follow-up is getting the new believer into good Christian fellowship. What will happen if the person you are following up has some social problems that limit his ability to develop good relationships with other Christians? It is obvious that his social problems will cause some spiritual problems as time goes by. It is therefore important that you are able to detect and deal with social problems as one step to seeing real growth in the spiritual side of a person's life.

Let's pursue this example further. The new Christian with whom you are working has a problem which is socially restricting. Your purpose in helping him with this problem is not so much to develop a well-polished individual, but rather to help him develop qualities to aid him in having fellowship with other Christians. There are various ways to help someone who is shy. If you have had this problem, show the new Christian what God has revealed to you from His Word to help you deal with it. Just to sit down with him in a follow-up visit and tell him he must get to know people and that God doesn't want him to be shy won't usually solve the problem. It is much more effective to show the new Christian how to do something about his problem and help him actually encounter other people.

Perhaps the person you are following up is blunt, loud, or turns others off. The best thing to do is to sit down with him and tell him his behavior offends other people. Often a person doesn't realize the reaction of others toward his behavior. He has developed a manner of social behavior which he practices, never realizing how it bothers other people. You might also work out some prearranged signal to tell the person when he is becoming offensive, or when he is saying something that should not be said. You do not need to be an expert on social graces to help the new Christian relate to the group.

Perhaps the new Christian needs counseling on family problems. I remember the home situation of one teen-ager I was following up. The father came home drunk every night and beat up the family. Obviously you need to do more than just go over follow-up appointments with such a person. This fellow needed help to face his problems. To really begin to help a new Christian you must get to know more about the circumstances he faces. In this case the new Christian had neglected his devotions. It turned out he wanted to take time for them, but because of the family situation at home he was unable to do so. If I had kept urging him to have devotions without seeking to help this complicating problem, I would only have succeeded in creating frustration and wide communication gaps.

Perhaps the person you are working with has hygiene problems. Who is going to tell him if you don't? You should work toward developing the type of relationship with him where you will be able to give guidance in areas which might prove embarrassing. Your purpose is not to pry, but rather to help him grow in Christ. You are trying to help him become a confident individual. I'm not advocating that you inquire into areas where you are not wanted. Don't force a person to tell you everything. Just be open and receptive. All of this will contribute to developing an attitude of acceptance and mutual confidence, which will greatly aid you in the area of spiritual follow-up. As the new Christian develops confidence in you, he is going to believe more and more of what you say and accept it as authority. This is especially true when it comes to solving problems.

Perhaps the new Christian has a financial difficulty. Maybe his problem is an unworkable budget, since many people just don't know how to make one. Bitter experience taught me how to budget. Perhaps he is going through all kinds of struggle and worry as a result of this problem. To sit down and talk to him about worry will not help him if you can't get to the root of his problem. Again the point here is the need to see each individual as a total person and not just address yourself to one segment of his life.

Remember What He Tells You

Another factor in developing relationships is to remember what the new Christian shares with you. Both as a student and as a full-time Christian worker, I had some bitter experiences in this area. I had a habit of forgetting what people told me. When I was working as a staff member with Campus Crusade for Christ, there were times when I met with someone and would forget what his major was in college, or what courses he was taking. This can really become embarrassing. People begin to think you don't really care.

After being embarrassed several times, I developed an easy method of storing information that really helped me with this problem. I began to carry a 3 x 5 card to fill out after I finished meeting with a person. I would jot down all the important information he had told me. Before the next time we met I reviewed the 3 x 5 card. In the initial stages of working with a person it is extremely important to have that information. I mention this problem because it has happened to me and it may well happen to you. If you have a bad memory, start writing things down. People don't usually get turned off by this. It even reassures them that you are concerned enough about them to want to remember what they say.

Be a Leader As Well As a Friend

The next factor in developing a relationship with a new Christian is the need to strike the right balance between being both spiritual leader and friend. In the midst of all this emphasis on friendship and relationship, it is easy to sidestep being a leader. None of us really wants the responsibility of being a leader. We would much rather avoid having to help a new Christian grow in Christ. We prefer to sidestep our responsibility to confront a new believer involved in a sin; we try to put all the responsibility on the Lord to reprove and convict him. This takes the pressure away from us. It is much easier, but much less effective, to remain nonauthoritative in our relationship.

This is one side of the coin. It is also important to realize that it is possible to become too authoritative or problem-oriented. It is best to deal with only one problem at a time, which is quite enough to keep a person busy. Be careful not to make your whole relationship one of constantly telling the new Christian what he is doing wrong. It is much better to have a healthy balance in your relationship of mutual encouragement, sharing of spiritual truths, and counseling. If you keep it balanced you won't create a negative atmosphere of defeat and legalism.

Fig. 9 Keeping Balance in Follow-up

You won't always get positive response from the new Christian as you attempt to be his spiritual leader. There will be negative reactions to deal with as well. You must show him that negative reactions are sinful. If you have been presenting the Word of God to him to point out a particular problem, and he rebels against it, his rebellion is not against you but against God's will. If, however, you have been obnoxious or tried to push too many things on him at one time, then his reaction is your fault. Achieving a good balance is essential.

Another important element in being an effective leader is to deal with problems when they arise and in the order of their priority. There may be more than one obvious problem at a particular time. Deal with the one most crucial to his spiritual growth. If you will deal with problems when they first arise, you keep them from becoming major. This honest dealing with problems helps the new Christian develop good habits of Christian living. If, however, you wait too long to deal with a problem, the new Christian will have developed a bad habit. When this happens, it becomes harder to deal with and gain victory over. I am convinced problem-solving is a crucial part of follow-up and discipleship. Thus this book will focus more on problem-solving in chapter 5. I hope you will begin to see that it does play an important role and that you are called to be a spiritual leader who gives direction to people in solving their problems. Ask God to help you be an effective friend and leader to the new Christian He has entrusted into your care.

Conclusion

Having spent this time discussing the role of relationship in effective personal follow-up, we are ready to move on to the more practical how-to's of this work. My big fear is that readers are looking, or might begin to look, upon personal follow-up as merely a process of transferring spiritual truth, rather than the communication of a life. I hope this chapter prevents such a misconception. It is important to develop a meaningful total relationship with a new Christian before effective personal follow-up can take place.

To summarize, when developing relationships make sure you are creating an atmosphere of concern and accepting love. Develop your relationship so that discussing spiritual things is the natural, not awkward, thing to do. Be patient and stick to it when seeking to build this relationship. It will take time and all relationships will not grow at the same rate. Be disciplined in spending quality time with the new Christian. Time is an important ingredient in the developing of an effective relationship. Make sure that you're aware of and dealing with problems in all aspects of a new Christian's life. Guard against becoming too narrow in your perspective on what is involved in real growth.

Develop an effective way of remembering what the new Christian tells you. Finally, strike a good balance between friendship and leadership. If these things are true in your relationship with a new Christian, it will not be long before you will see true effectiveness developing in your personal follow-up ministry.

> *For if they fall, one will lift up his fellow;*
> *but woe to him who is alone when he falls and*
> *has not another to lift him up (Eccl. 4:10).*

Notes

1 Coleman, *Master Plan of Evangelism,* pp.38-49.

4

Planning
For Follow-up

A Comprehensive Study

Now we are ready to turn to the more practical "how-to" aspects of follow-up. My stress thus far in this book has been on the importance of life impartation in addition to information communication. I hope the point has been made and you are in basic agreement with it. If this is true, then we are ready to turn our attention to the practical expansion of the topic of personal follow-up. The two most basic and commonly asked questions I encounter in the various conferences at which I speak could be stated as follows: (1) Where are we headed in follow-up? and (2) How do we get there from here? It is to these questions and related ones that I will address myself in this chapter.

GOALS OF FOLLOW-UP

Abraham Lincoln said in 1858, "If we could first know where we are, and whither we are tending, we could better judge

71

what to do and how to do it." The truth of this statement is still applicable today. We must know where we are headed. Another quote I heard some time ago also applies in this area. It goes something like this: "People don't plan to fail, they fail to plan." I don't know who said this, but he certainly was perceptive. It is imperative that we plan ahead when it comes to something as important as personally following up a new Christian. You must know where you are going and how you are going to get there.

The first step in formulating a good plan of personal follow-up involves setting goals. What are the biblical goals of a personal follow-up ministry? I would like to propose six goals that I have found important as a first step in solving this problem. The goals will be discussed in the order of their probable achievement.

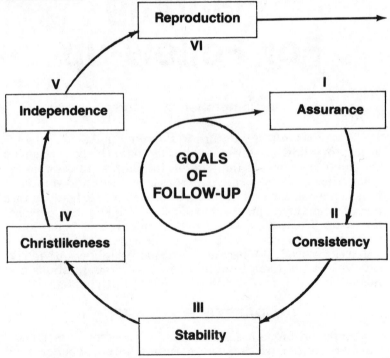

Fig. 10 Basic Goals of Follow-up

1. Assurance of Salvation and Standing in Christ

It is essential that a new Christian receive assurance of his salvation and some basic teaching on his standing in Christ. If this is not achieved first, it will avail little to go on to other areas in follow-up. If the new believer is unable to gain an assurance of his salvation, this problem must be dealt with at the outset. Chapter 5 will examine this problem in more detail.

2. Consistency in the Fundamentals

After assurance of salvation has been received, you are ready to move on to the next goal. There needs to be an application in the new believer's life of many fundamental truths of how to grow in Christ. He must develop a disciplined devotional life. This is vitally important and sets up the preconditions for a growing, more intimate walk with Christ. The new believer also needs to become actively involved in dynamic Christian fellowship and be consistent in his involvement. Closely tied to this need is the importance of involvement in a good church. He should have an on-going program of memorizing God's Word, and he needs some basic training in outreach as well. These and similar factors are what I am referring to as fundamentals. Chapter 1 also elaborated on this point.

3. Stability in Basic Doctrine

An extremely important goal is solid grounding in Bible doctrine. The Word of God often refers to the dangers involved in not being well grounded in doctrine. For one example, note Paul's warning in Ephesians 4:14: "Then we will no longer be *infants*, tossed back and forth by the waves, and blown here and there by every wind of teaching and by the cunning and craftiness of men in their deceitful scheming." This verse makes a clear statement on the relationship between maturity and stability. Establishing a Christian solidly based in Bible doctrine, a basic goal in follow-up, may be achieved through group and personal teaching of the Word of God.

4. Developing Christlikeness

An obvious goal in personal follow-up is the development

of the fruit of the Spirit in the life of a believer. You seek to make Christ seen increasingly in his life. This will be the product of both teaching and counseling on the basic ingredients of the Spirit-filled life. Examine and meditate on Paul's goal in his personal follow-up as he expresses it in Galatians 4:19: "My dear children, for whom I am again in the pains of childbirth *until Christ is formed in you!*" It must be your heart-felt desire to see this occur. Remember, as was discussed in chapter 2, you will only reproduce what you have attained in your own life. Like begets like.

5. Independently Applying and Benefiting From the Word of God

Another important goal in personal follow-up is to develop a growing independence in the life of a new believer. By this I mean helping him grow to the point where he is able to make application of the Word of God on his own. You want him to begin to use the Bible when he seeks to help others. The way to best accomplish this goal is through training him to use the Bible to solve problems. Make him independently dependent, i.e., independent of you and dependent on God.

6. Reproducing Previous Goals in Lives of Other People

A basic goal of all personal follow-up should be the production of multipliers. To achieve this goal is the focus of the training in this book. You should always have the production of multipliers in the back of your mind when you do follow-up.

It is important to have set goals for your work in follow-up. I hope these six have stimulated your thinking and motivated you to get involved. But knowing these goals and achieving them are obviously different things. The emphasis from this point on will be to show you how to achieve these goals in the life of the person God has privileged you to follow up. There are three steps that must be taken before you will be able to achieve the goals of your follow-up ministry. First, you must define in more detail the content of the goals. Second, you must develop a curriculum to insure the inclusion of all needed content. Third, you must develop a planned schedule of instruction in which to confront the new Christian with the content. It is to these steps we now turn.

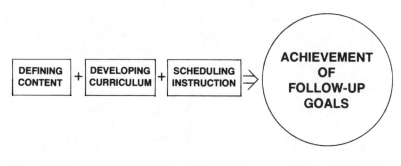

Fig. 11 Steps to Achieving Goals

FOLLOW-UP CONTENT

The first step in achieving the goals of follow-up involves defining in more detail the content of follow-up as contained within these goals. The content includes the many topics you cover while going through personal follow-up with an individual. All of the topics needed to achieve the goals of follow-up will align with one of three general areas of training. These are as follows:

1. *Devotional Area* – This is the topic area of personal follow-up training related to the growth and development of Christlikeness in a new believer's life.

2. *Doctrinal Area* – This is the topic area of personal follow-up training related to the impartation of biblical, doctrinal, and related knowledge in the new believer's life.

3. *Discipleship Area* – This is the topic area of personal follow-up training related to developing expertise in Christian service in the areas of witnessing, teaching, and follow-up in a new believer's life.

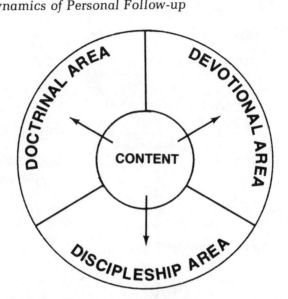

Fig. 12 Defining Content of Follow-up

In spite of the fact that these areas overlap to a certain extent, this threefold division will enable us to be more definite in our planning of a complete program of personal follow-up. This threefold division also is helpful in providing ways to gauge more accurately progress in the new Christian's life. Using this criteria we have something definite against which to check a person's progress.

Devotional Area

It is necessary to examine in more depth some of the curriculum that must be followed to help a new believer develop in the area of Christlikeness. The following is a list of fifteen topics that must be covered in a total program of personal follow-up in the devotional area. While not exhaustive, it is comprehensive. A suggested way of presenting many of these topics to a new Christian is included in the series of suggested follow-up appointments in Appendix 1 of this book.

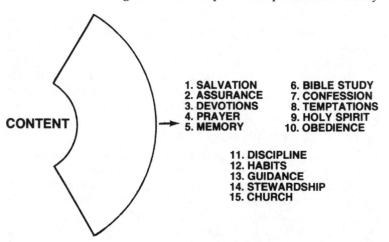

1. SALVATION   6. BIBLE STUDY
2. ASSURANCE   7. CONFESSION
3. DEVOTIONS   8. TEMPTATIONS
4. PRAYER   9. HOLY SPIRIT
CONTENT → 5. MEMORY 10. OBEDIENCE

11. DISCIPLINE
12. HABITS
13. GUIDANCE
14. STEWARDSHIP
15. CHURCH

Fig. 13 Topic Content: Devotional Area

1. Salvation. This is the primary area of teaching because everything begins with this. Often when you initiate personal follow-up with someone, you will find he has never actually received Christ. Since this is an ever-present possibility, elaborate more on the true meaning of salvation before you begin to teach him about growing in Christ. Review the gospel often during the first few weeks of follow-up with a new believer. Assign reading that elaborates on the meaning of salvation. Be certain the person has indeed repented and received Christ before you go further into follow-up. Appendix 2 gives some suggested readings for this topic. Chapter 5 explains how to help someone who doesn't clearly understand the gospel.

2. Assurance of Salvation. As was mentioned in the discussion on goals of personal follow-up, assurance of salvation must be given to a new Christian. He needs to be sure where he stands in Christ. Follow-up Appointment I in Appendix 1 covers this topic and should give you some insight and suggestions. Chapter 5 will explain how to help someone with difficulties in this area.

3. Devotions. It is important that the new believer receive instruction in developing a meaningful devotional life. This should come early in your personal follow-up teaching. It is in the daily time alone with God, in the study of His Word, that a new Christian begins to discover the dynamic of the Bible. He begins to understand God's voice and direction and learns to commune with God in his heart. It is important that he become consistent in this area of life. Follow-up Appointment II in Appendix 1 covers this topic in greater depth.

4. Prayer. It is also necessary to develop communication with God in the area of prayer. A new believer needs to be taught what prayer is, why it is needed, and how to use it. He needs training to develop adequately in this area of his life. Example is highly effective in communicating this truth. This is the way the Lord worked with His disciples. He taught them the importance of prayer by example. See Mark 1:35; Luke 5:16; Matthew 14:23. Follow-up Appointment 5 in Appendix 1 deals with this topic.

5. Memorizing Scripture. Memorizing Scripture is vitally important in the life of a new believer. This is how the Word of God becomes implanted in his life. There is a direct relationship between the amount of victory in a Christian's life and the amount of Scripture laid up in his heart (Ps. 119:11). Obviously, this is not the only factor in victory, but it is significant. Memorizing Scripture develops discipline in the new believer's life as well as increasing his confidence in knowing the Word of God. An excellent memory program is offered by the Navigators.[1]

6. Bible Study Methods. In the course of follow-up one must do more than just encourage devotional study of God's Word. A new Christian also needs training on how to *inductively* study God's Word.[2] This will enable the new Christian to grow more independent of you and more systematic in his knowledge of the Bible. It makes the Bible a more usable tool for the new believer.

7. Confession of Sin. The new believer must learn what to do about unconfessed sin in his life. If we miss this vital instruction, many will go around for years with an unnecessary load of guilt and frustration on their shoulders. The truths of 1 John, Psalm 32, Psalm 38, and other Scriptures must be clearly communicated to the new Christian. An excellent book on this topic is *How to Experience God's Love and Forgiveness* by Bill Bright.[3]

8. *Dealing with Temptations.* This is the other side of the coin introduced in point 7. It is concerned with preventing sin in the first place. A new believer must know the steps to victorious Christian living and how to handle temptation when it comes along. Most books of Spirit-filled living deal with this topic. Appendix 2 contains a listing of helpful books in this area, and Follow-up Appointment VII in Appendix 1 also deals with this topic.

9. *Spirit-Filled Life.* One of the key truths of the Christian life involves the dynamics of Spirit-filled living. Christ lives His resurrected life in and through us in the power of the Holy Spirit. See the books listed in Appendix 2 for suggested readings on this topic. Follow-up Appointment IV in Appendix 1 is concerned with this topic.

10. *Obedience.* It will be necessary to impress upon a growing Christian the importance of obedience, for obedience and discipline play a large role in developing godliness in a person's life. Follow-up Appointment VI in Appendix 1 deals more in depth with this topic.

11. *God's Discipline.* Much space in Scripture is devoted to elaborating on the Lord's discipline in our lives. Hebrews 12, for example, goes into much detail on this subject. It is important for a new Christian to realize that since he is God's son and God loves him, he will be disciplined to help him grow in Christ. It is important to explain this truth to a new believer and caution him about rebellion against God's discipline.[4]

12. *Developing Godly Habits of Living.* Here we emphasize the need in the new Christian's life for righteousness. This is the putting off of the old nature with its habits and the putting on of the new nature (Eph. 4:20-22). A most excellent booklet on this topic is *Godliness Through Discipline* by Jay Adams.[5]

13. Knowing God's Will. The need to understand God's guidance in one's life is an important aspect in follow-up. It is vital that a new Christian learn to find God's will in every area of his life. Follow-up Appointment VII in Appendix 1 deals with this topic.

14. Stewardship. It is important for a new Christian to understand the biblical teaching on stewardship. This includes not only possessions, but also talents, time, and life. We were "bought with a price" and are under obligation to serve God in all things.

15. Church Involvement. The church plays a vital role in the life of a new believer. It is extremely important that a new Christian quickly establish bonds of Christian fellowship. These will strengthen him and greatly stimulate his growth. This is the topic of Follow-up Appointment III in Appendix 1.

In this whole discussion of the devotional area curriculum, it is important to relate again that this is an area of Christian nurture particularly effective when communicated on a one-to-one basis. The follow-up appointments in Appendix 1 deal with the majority of these fifteen topic areas. These appointment guides are written in such a way that you should have little difficulty in learning to use them. Much more will be said in chapter 7 on the specifics of working one-to-one in personal follow-up. Refer back and forth between these chapters to gain insights into developing an adequate follow-up program. We are now ready to move on to the second area of curriculum in personal follow-up.

Doctrinal Area

Certain questions often arise in discussions I have led on the topic of personal follow-up: "How much doctrine does this new Christian need to know to become established in his faith?" "How much of a systematic knowledge of the Word of God does this new Christian need to gain?" "How much should this new Christian know in the area of apologetics?" These and similar questions are important to answer in the development of a total program of personal follow-up.

Another question involving doctrinal knowledge pertains to its mode of communication. What is the most effective way to impart this type of knowledge? For the topics covered under curriculum of the devotional area of follow-up, the most effective method involves personal instruction. Does the same hold true for doctrinal teaching? I believe the answer to this question is no. Experience has taught me that it is the group teaching time where doctrine is best communicated. There are two basic reasons for this. First, the nature of the topics contained in this division make it more difficult and awkward to communicate on a one-on-one level. You would have to lecture almost entirely, and this is not desirable on a personal level. There is little room for dialogue in doctrinal instruction. Secondly, there is a need to know far more than you are communicating when you teach doctrine. You must be sensitive to error. It takes a long time to develop the knowledge necessary to teach in this area. Remember the warning in James 3:1.

Returning to the initial questions, how much information do we need to be sure a new Christian knows to be stable in his faith? There are four basic areas of knowledge important in developing mature believers.

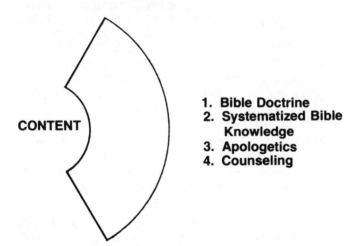

CONTENT

1. **Bible Doctrine**
2. **Systematized Bible Knowledge**
3. **Apologetics**
4. **Counseling**

Fig. 14 Topic Content: Doctrinal Area

Doctrine: Refers to the need of a basic level of systematized doctrinal knowledge in a new believer's life.

Systematized Biblical Knowledge: Refers to the need of a systematic knowledge of the content of the Word of God.

Apologetics: Refers to the knowledge needed in the area of making a defense of the Christian faith.

Counseling: Refers to the knowledge needed in knowing how to use the Word of God to solve problems.

These four areas of knowledge are essential to the growth of a new Christian. Let's examine each more closely.

1. *Doctrine.* There are a number of basic doctrines of the faith a new Christian should be learning. The priority question, i.e., the order in which we teach them is answered by dealing first with those which are most often misunderstood or perverted by cults. You may assume the new Christian will probably soon run into conflict in these areas of doctrine. The following is a list of basic doctrines he should know.

1. *The Trinity.* The new Christian should be able to defend this doctrine. He should know some supporting illustrations and the necessity of adhering to this truth. This is a focal point of attack by cults and apostasy.

2. *Deity of Christ.* The fact that Jesus is God is an all-important truth in comprehending the Atonement. A person should have a basic understanding of the God-man concept and know how to scripturally defend the doctrine.

3. *Salvation.* A person needs to have a clear understanding of the Atonement, the role of repentance and saving faith in conversion, and the meaning of justification. He must be able to deal with attempts to teach a salvation by any other means than grace.

4. *Sanctification.* A new Christian needs to have an understanding of the dynamics of growth in Christ.

This will be necessary to guard against extremes of teaching when it comes to abundant, victorious Christian living.

5. *Satan/Demons.* A new Christian needs to know the biblical teachings on Satan and how to gain victory over him. New believers need to know about demons and the occult. It is necessary to have a broad understanding in these areas to prevent extremes arising from either too much or too little concern.

6. *Church.* It is important that a new Christian understand something of the diversity of teaching on the church, its history, purpose, policy, and end. This will prevent much extremism.

2. Systematized Bible Knowledge. It is also important that a new believer have a minimum level of systematic biblical knowledge. There will be much disagreement concerning what this level should be, although the following would be a minimum standard in my opinion. The new Christian should learn the location of all the books in the Bible. This would seem to be an obvious achievement, but I have found many adults who have great difficulty finding anything in the Bible. Another basic need is a general understanding of the themes of the New Testament books. This will do much to help a person use the Bible more effectively and will guard against some extremes in emphasis. A program study should be begun to learn the themes of all the chapters in the New Testament books. Learning one Gospel and the Book of Romans would be a good start. A knowledge of the authorship and background for each book would also be a useful tool for the growing Christian. One note at this point: I am discussing goals in follow-up to be achieved over a period of time. I am not referring to things to be accomplished in a matter of weeks, but rather over months and even years. Jesus spent nearly three years with His disciples. Perhaps three years would be a good time to aim for the achievement of these goals.

3. Apologetics. A knowledge of some basic apologetics is also helpful for a growing Christian. This will enable him to become a much more effective tool in the hands of the Lord and will serve to give him much more stability in his faith. The following is a list of what I consider minimum knowledge in the area of apologetics. A list of good apologetical books will be given in Appendix 2.

1. Inspiration of Scripture
2. Proofs for the Resurrection
3. Errors of cults
4. Errors of other faiths
5. Philosophy and faith
6. Science and the Bible

4. Counseling. The last topic in the curriculum of the doctrinal area deals with biblical counseling. An adequate discussion of this topic goes beyond the bounds of this book, so I will limit our discussion here to identifying the need and content of counseling knowledge. Appendix 2 lists further reading on this topic for those who are interested. The need is to help the new Christian use the Bible as a problem-solving source for his life. Also he should learn to use the Bible to help others solve their problems. He should gain knowledge on how to deal with some of the most common difficulties a Christian encounters, including anger, worry, depression, jealousy, thought life, and moral problems.

As you provide opportunities for a new Christian to gain knowledge in these areas, you will surely see a growing change in that person's life. Take pains to insure that this occurs in the life of the person you are following up. Let's now turn our attention on the third area of content.

Discipleship Area

The last area of content to be examined in this discussion involves the topics of training for outreach. I have labeled this "Discipleship." The question we seek to answer here is: What do I need to do with a growing Christian to insure a multiplication of my training? This question is being answered throughout this book, so I will not deal with it exhaustively at this point. However, I would like to give you a summary of the topics included in outreach training. These will show you what you need to communicate if you want to see multiplication. The how-to's of communicating this training will be dealt with later. The following is a minimal list of seven training topics for personal development in a new believer's life.

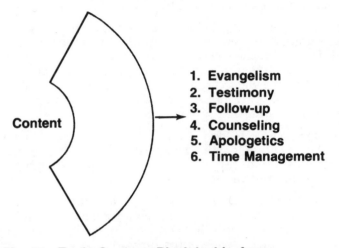

1. Evangelism
2. Testimony
3. Follow-up
4. Counseling
5. Apologetics
6. Time Management

Content

Fig. 15 Topic Content: Discipleship Area

1. Knowledge of How to Share the Faith. It is important that you go beyond simply challenging a person to share his faith; you must also train him to do it. This can be done either personally or by encouraging him to attend a training conference in evangelism.

2. Developing an Evangelistic Testimony. One of the most effective tools in evangelistic outreach is the use of a testimony. A personal testimony relating the change Christ made in a life is a powerful force in lending credibility to the gospel. It is important that a person has thought through ahead of time what he will say. Follow-up Appointment VIII in Appendix 1 will aid you in this area of training.

3. Follow-up Training. When the person you are following

up begins to become serious about involvement in evangelistic outreach, inevitably he will have fruit. At this point he should have some basic training on how to give a new Christian assurance of salvation and help him begin to grow in Christ. Having him read this book and showing him how to use some of the appointments in Appendix 1 should help in this area.

4. *Biblical Counseling.* When a person begins to follow-up others, he should also begin to learn how to deal biblically with problems in the life of a new believer. Both your personal problem-solving with him and your suggestions for guided readings will enable you to train him to work effectively in this area. Have him take advantage of all good training programs available in counseling and problem-solving.

5. *Working Knowledge of Apologetics.* As I have already examined the role of apologetics, I will just mention it in passing here. Its application to discipleship is obvious. A list of good books in this area is given in Appendix 2.

6. *Time Management.* It is important that a growing Christian be trained in proper time management for he will soon be running into problems with the use of his time. Teaching on priorities and training in scheduling time are needed.[6]

This brings us to the end of the study on the content of follow-up. We have examined goals for follow-up and looked into the content of teaching and training contained within these goals. The question probably going through your mind is, Where do you go from here? You might be thinking that the work of follow-up is much too complex and you are afraid to try it. You might even be thinking you will never be able to accomplish all these goals in the life of a new Christian. Perhaps this content I have put forth has not been totally achieved as yet in your own life. Well, take heart. Remember that God's biggest problem is your lack of availability. If you will make yourself available to Him for this work of personal follow-up, in spite of your fears and limitations, God will use you. One of the solutions to a portion of your fears is knowing how to make sure all these topics in personal follow-up (i.e., Devotional, Doctrinal, and

Discipleship) will be accomplished and applied. The answer lies in developing a planned curriculum for the new believer's life. It is possible to plan for a new believer's growth and check it accurately if you have a plan. This brings us to the second step in this chapter.

DEVELOPING THE CURRICULUM

At this point it should be obvious that it is one thing to know the truths needing explanation in following up a new Christian, yet it is something else to know *how* to cover them. You must develop a clear method of communicating truths to new Christians. As mentioned earlier, for some of the topics I have suggested ways of covering them in the ten follow-up appointments found in Appendix 1. Thus you will already have some knowledge of how to cover the more important truths. By studying the follow-up appointments in Appendix 1, you will have a guide for developing other topics identified as important.

A second aspect of developing the curriculum for follow-up is to determine what you will cover personally with a new believer and what you will make sure he receives from other sources, i.e., personal study and group teaching. As I mentioned earlier, some topics in follow-up are covered much more effectively in group teaching than in one-on-one meetings, while others are best understood through the vehicle of personal study. The following is a sample of such a breakdown.

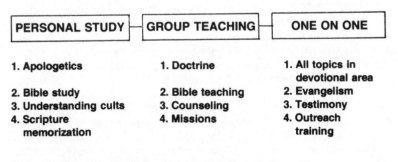

PERSONAL STUDY	GROUP TEACHING	ONE ON ONE
1. Apologetics	1. Doctrine	1. All topics in devotional area
2. Bible study	2. Bible teaching	2. Evangelism
3. Understanding cults	3. Counseling	3. Testimony
4. Scripture memorization	4. Missions	4. Outreach training

Fig. 16 Sample Division of Instruction

Once you have the curriculum developed, you are ready to begin to implement it in following up new Christians. This brings us to step 3 in this chapter.

SCHEDULING INSTRUCTION

> Commit your work to the Lord, and your plans
> will be established (Prov. 16:3).

We must work toward goals and evaluate progress. It is important to schedule your training of a new believer and keep accurate records of his progress. Personal follow-up does not just happen; we must plan for it. We will never achieve good results if we are sloppy and haphazard in our methods. Remember, the God we serve is well organized. Examine 1 Corinthians 14:33: "For God is not a God of disorder, but of peace." If you are disorganized and without a plan for your personal follow-up of new believers, then you are not really following our Lord's example.

Your scheduling of follow-up and evaluation of its progress can best be accomplished with two planning tools. The first is a long-range follow-up planning sheet and the second is a follow-up progress report sheet. Let's examine the use of these tools in more depth.

The long-range planning sheet is for scheduling and planning the overall follow-up instruction of a new believer. This instruction includes both the topics you cover on a personal level and the topics he covers in group instruction and personal study. It is important that you gain an overview in the area of goals. Without this overview, it will be hard to settle on priorities of instruction. It is also easy to leave out vital instruction. Once you settle on a plan of approach, it will probably remain quite similar for everyone you work with. You develop this plan based on what you know about a new believer and his needs. The long-range planning sheet covers a one-year period and is divided into two-month increments. Figure 17 gives you an example of the training schedule I follow in my own ministry of personal follow-up. I hope it will be of assistance in demonstrating how to utilize this tool.

LONG-RANGE
FOLLOW-UP PLANNING SHEET

MO.	ONE-ON-ONE	GROUP	PERSONAL STUDY
1-2	1. Follow-up Appoint-ments (Appendix 1)	1. New Believers Class 2. Bible Exposition	1. Devotions 2. Books on Assurance
3-4	1. Follow-up Appoint-ments (Appendix 1) 2. Training in Evangelism 3. Scripture Memory Program	1. Basic Doctrine Class 2. Bible Exposi-tion	1. Devotions 2. Books of Growth 3. Scripture Memory
5-6	1. Training in Evangelism 2. Developing a Testimony 3. Inductive Bible Study	1. Basic Doctrine Class 2. Bible Exposition	1. Devotions 2. Books on Doctrine 3. Scripture Memory
7-8	1. Training in Follow-up 2. Counseling As Needed	1. Bible Exposition 2. Evangelism Training	1. Devotions 2. Inductive Bible Study 3. Scripture Memory 4. Books on Witnessing
9-10	1. Counseling As Needed	1. Bible Exposition 2. Counseling Training	1. Devotions 2. Inductive Study 3. Scripture Memory 4. Books on Apologetics
11-12	1. Counseling As Needed	1. Bible Exposition 2. Counseling Training	1. Devotions 2. Inductive Study 3. Scripture Memory 4. Books on Miscellaneous Topics

Fig. 17

The follow-up progress report sheet is the means of putting your long-range plan for follow-up into action. The progress report sheet keeps track of dates of instruction, turning points in spiritual growth, and comments on the progress in the new believer's growth. This report form is especially important during the first six months of a new Christian's life in Christ. If a person is well cared for in this critical period, the chance of lasting fruitfulness and multiplication is greatly increased. It is your responsibility to know at all times where an individual stands in his relationship to Christ. I have given an example of this form in Figure 18. You will probably find that you must use several of these sheets in the course of personal follow-up with a new believer to keep track of his growth. It would be wise to invest in a file folder for each person you have ever worked with and keep it up-to-date. Perhaps every six weeks you should up-date it, even when you are past the stage of consistent, one-on-one follow-up with an individual. Again, it should be your goal to be well organized in your follow-up ministry.

CONCLUSION

We have examined many concepts in this chapter. Hopefully, it has not proved to be confusing. It is important to set goals for your follow-up. If you are not aiming at anything, you will accomplish little. Therefore, your goals must be specific. It is also essential that you define the content of personal follow-up. You should know what you are seeking to accomplish in a new believer's life, and you should be clear as to what his needs really are.

The remaining chapters of this book will deal with the problems encountered in the implementation of effective follow-up and the how-to's of making multipliers out of new Christians.

FOLLOW-UP
PROGRESS REPORT SHEET

NAME _____ AGE _____

ADDRESS _____ PHONE _____

TOPIC	DATE OF MEETING	COMMENTS

(continue form on back of page)

KEY TURNING POINTS AND DATES

___1. Assurance ___/___/___

___2. Consistent Devotions ___/___/___

___3. Involved in Church ___/___/___

___4. Witnessed ___/___/___

___5. Consistent Witness ___/___/___

___6. Following-up ___/___/___

___7. Saw Fruit ___/___/___

___8. Reproduced Himself ___/___/___

Fig. 18

The Dynamics of Personal Follow-up

Notes

[1] This memory course offered by the Navigators is a helpful aid in helping the new Christian to begin to memorize Scripture. The cost of this course is $5.00 and may be obtained by writing for it in care of: Navigators, P.O. Box 1659, Colorado Springs, CO 80901.

[2] An excellent book on Bible study methods: Oletta Wald, *Joy of Discovery* (Minneapolis, MN: Bible Banner Press, 1956).

[3] Bill Bright, *How to Experience God's Love and Forgiveness* (Arrowhead Springs, CA: Campus Crusade for Christ, 1971).

[4] Hebrews 12 teaches us some important truths about God's discipline. It tells us that (1) God will discipline us; (2) God's discipline is proof of His love and our sonship; (3) we are not to rebel against it; and (4) it will produce growth in our lives. It is also important to understand some of the methods God employs in disciplining us. Scripture teaches that God will use the following to bring us to repentance: (a) a guilty conscience — conviction (2 Tim. 3:6; John 16:8); (b) Guilt and loss of peace — depression (Pss. 32;38); (c) psychosomatic illness — (Pss. 32; 38); (d) Physical illness (James 5:16; 1 Cor. 11:30). This is not an exhaustive list, and c and d are not always caused by discipline. More work needs to be done on this topic.

[5] Jay Adams, *Godliness Through Discipline* (Nutley, NJ: Presbyterian and Reformed Publishing Co., 1971).

[6] Three helpful books on the topic of time management are:
John W Alexander, *Managing Our Work* (Downers Grove, IL: IVP, 1972).
Edward R. Dayton, *Tools for Time Management* (Grand Rapids: Zondervan, 1974).
Ted W. Engstrom and Alec Mackenzie, *Managing Your Time* (Grand Rapids: Zondervan, 1967).

5

Dealing With Common Problems Encountered In Personal Follow-up

Now that we have examined the content of personal follow-up and discussed how to plan for implementing this program in the life of the new believer, we are ready to discuss practical considerations. Regardless of how much you have prepared or how much you try to avoid them, you are going to run into problems in your personal follow-up ministry with new Christians. Not everyone is going to respond in a positive manner to your program of Christian nurture. How are you going to deal with the problems you encounter in follow-up? Are you going to pass over them, as many people choose to do? Will you deal with the problems that arise as you feel led at the time? If you answer yes to either of these options, you are in for a frustrating time in your personal follow-up ministry. You are going to find that neither offers a satisfactory solution to your problem. You cannot merely pass over problems and hope they will go away. Instead of going away, they usually grow larger and more ominous. If you wait to think about how to deal with problems until they arise, you will become painfully aware of how limited you are in the area of biblical counseling. The best solution is to prepare ahead of time to meet any problem you are likely to encounter. This will not only better equip you for effective personal follow-up, but it will also greatly increase your confidence.

The question that arises in your mind at this point probably focuses on where can you go for the answers to follow-up problems you might face. This is a legitimate question. As I began to do personal follow-up, early in my ministry, I was faced with the same problem. I found no place to go for these answers. This forced me to do much of my problem-solving by trial and error — definitely not the way to do personal follow-up! The bad experiences of this period of my life greatly motivated me to take precautions against a repeat of this problem for others. For the past several years I have spent much time in discussion with fellow staff, other Christian workers, and involved laymen, seeking to identify the most common problems in follow-up and determine the most effective ways of dealing with them. This chapter is an outgrowth of that work. The problems of this chapter are not so much counseling problems as they are hindrances to consistent Christian growth. I hope that by dealing with these problems in this chapter I can save you frustration and heartache. Space will limit my discussion, but I trust sufficient depth will be given to insure applicability to your personal follow-up ministry.

As I mentioned previously, in my discussions with my staff, fellow Christian workers, and laymen, I found certain problems to be occurring frequently. I have since compiled a list of problems in the order of their frequency of occurence in follow-up. This is in no way the last word in this area, but rather reflects the findings of those with whom I have had contact. Perhaps you have found other problems equally frequent or maybe you would reverse the order in which I have listed them. This in no way reflects disagreement, but rather different experiences. It is an area where I am open to further discussion. The following is the list of the most common problems in the order of their frequency.

The new Christian:

1. Is unwilling to meet with you for follow-up.
2. Is unable to receive assurance of salvation.
3. Has continued problems with guilt in his life.
4. Has an undisciplined devotional life.
5. Is afraid to identify publicly with Christ.
6. Is involved in a weak or liberal church.
7. Faces strong family and peer opposition.
8. Cannot believe in the credibility of the person doing follow-up.
9. Encounters strong intellectual problems.
10. Goes to an extreme in some area of questionable doctrine or aspect of Christian living.

The rest of this chapter will concentrate on practical insights into dealing with these problems. I will examine possible causes and steps toward solution. It would be impossible to deal with every possible cause of a given problem, so my discussion will concentrate on the most common causes. The rest will be up to the direction of the Holy Spirit in your life and your own practical experience gained through working with people in personal follow-up who have these problems.

Problem 1: Unwillingness to Meet

This unwillingness to meet will be the biggest problem you will encounter. Many people who make a decision for Christ, either at a meeting or personal evangelism encounter, are strangely unresponsive to attempts at personal follow-up. This problem also surfaces at different points in the process of following up a new believer, not always just at the beginning of your work with him. I would like to offer some insights into its causes and some suggestions as to its solution, but I will freely admit there are many situations which do not fit into the analysis I am offering. Let's first examine possible causes.

My experience over the past years has shown me that one of the prime reasons for reluctance to meet is an insincere commitment. A better way of stating this is that the person probably isn't really a Christian. His commitment could have been insincere for several reasons. Maybe he prayed to receive Christ during a personal evangelism contact merely to get rid of the person sharing Christ. I find this happens often with those personal workers learning to share Christ who have not developed the sensitivity a more experienced Christian would have in evangelism. Sometimes a commitment made during an evangelistic service, program, or movie was purely an emotional response without the intellect and will entering into the transaction. In a case like this, the person did not really repent and receive Christ as Savior. A more extensive discussion of what is involved in true conversion will be given under the section dealing with those who lack assurance of their salvation. Although there are other possible reasons for an insincere commitment, the important truth to understand at this point is that this could be the problem lurking behind an unwillingness to meet for follow-up.

Another possible cause of an unwillingness to meet for follow-up lies in satanic opposition. A new believer is perhaps more vulnerable to Satan than at any other time in his life. It will be easy to cast all kinds of doubt into minds of new Christians. Satan will seek to make him feel foolish, question the validity of his belief, tempt him to keep his decision quiet. And he will use many other deceptive devices to hinder the new Christian's development in Christ. Since this is a strong possibility in any unwillingness to meet, you must be ready to deal with it. Remember the warning in 1 Peter 5:8: "Be self-controlled and alert. Your enemy the devil prowls around like a roaring lion looking for someone to devour." Your new Christian would make a good meal. You need to protect him. Remember the promise in James 4:7: " . . . Resist the devil, and he will flee from you."

Peer pressure also plays a strong role in the problem of unwillingness to meet for personal follow-up. As soon as a person makes a decision for Christ, his friends and relatives will try to hinder his growth, because they don't want him to change. Perhaps they will seek to monopolize his time so he can't have devotions and go to fellowship meetings. Or they will ridicule him and put him down if he continues to follow Christ. These and other pressures can do much to make a new Christian reconsider his commitment and cause him to balk at follow-up.

Sometimes the problem is simply a lack of understanding as to the purpose and need of follow-up. The new Christian simply doesn't understand why you want to meet with him. He has been "burned" many times by people who had ulterior motives in being nice to him and seeking to be his friend. Life has taught him not to trust people. If he is unsure about the purpose of follow-up, he is bound to have a certain degree of suspicion in his dealings with you. This could account for his reluctance to meet with you.

Although there are other possible causes for a new Christian's unwillingness to meet for follow-up, the ones discussed should give you a head start in understanding this problem. Let's move on to discovering some possible ways to solve this problem.

The place to begin is prayer. This is an effective tool for solution. We find Paul continually mentioning prayer for young Christians in his Epistles. Consistent intercession will do much to change a new believer's attitude. This truth is fundamental and will apply to all follow-up problems.

There is a second means of solving this problem. It is to stress the need for growth in the Christian life. I have found many people who mistakenly feel just receiving Christ is all that is involved in the Christian faith. When this is the case, they must be made to see that it is also necessary to grow in Christ. Explain to them that while they are "babes," they need someone to act as a parent to them, to feed, protect, and nurture them until they are strong enough to go it alone. This will often clear up the misconceptions as to why you are desiring to get together.

For those whom you suspect are not truly converted, it will be essential to cover the "will-intellect-emotion" aspect of true conversion. The next section will deal with this in more depth.

The most crucial point of all in dealing with this problem is to get the new Christian to level with you and honestly state why he doesn't desire follow-up. You won't be able to get the person to agree to follow-up in every case. But with a grasp of what I have just covered, you will experience above-average success. Continue to seek to get together, and don't let one, two, or even three setbacks discourage you. If after several times of seeking to meet for personal follow-up, you are still unsuccessful, then leave the door open to further contacts, but move on to someone else. As a basic minimum, at least try to get the new Christian involved in some kind of group fellowship even if he is unwilling to participate in personal work.

Problem 2: Lack of Assurance

The second major problem is the number of new Christians who seem to be unable to receive any assurance of salvation. Primarily I am talking about those who still don't have any assurance, even after you have gone over assurance verses in the follow-up appointment. I make this distinction to rule out those whose lack of assurance stems from a lack of knowledge. Most of the people who lack assurance gain it in the normal process of personal follow-up as they gain an increased knowledge of the promises of God. It is when this normal development of assurance does not occur that you have a problem. What do you do if this problem faces you in your personal follow-up of a new Christian?

The most probable reason a person persists in an attitude of lacking assurance is that he isn't really saved and has nothing to be assured about. You can explore this possibility in more detail by elaborating with this person on the basic components of true conversion. True conversion is made up of repentance and saving faith. Both repentance and saving faith have the elements of will, intellect, and emotion involved in them. It is up to you to make a simple explanation of this complex theological truth. The best way to make a simple explanation is to know as much as you can about this truth. I would advise some concentrated reading on this subject.[1] Below is a short summary of these truths, followed by a simple way to communicate them to the person lacking assurance.

1. *Repentance.* Repentance is an essential element in true conversion. In the evangelism of some in this present day it seems to at times be *understressed.* We know that repentance is important from the following verses:

> In the past God overlooked such ignorance, but now he commands all people everywhere to repent (Acts 17:30).

> This is what is written: The Christ will suffer and rise from the dead on the third day, and *repentance* and forgiveness of sins will be preached in his name to all nations, beginning at Jerusalem (Luke 24:46,47).

From these and other portions of Scripture, repentance is clearly shown to be a necessary part of true salvation. The question at this point is: What is repentance? A simple definition would be to describe repentance as a change or turning involving the intellect, emotions, and will.

Intellectually, repentance is a changed view of sin, self, and God. A person understands that sin is really wrong and that it matters to a holy God. (Most people will admit that they sin, but they feel it doesn't matter, since they think God marks on a curve.) A person views himself as guilty before God and recognizes that God is just in condemning him as a penalty for his sins. These are the changes that occur in the intellect during true repentance and are reflected in the following verses: Psalm 51:3-5; Job 42:56; Luke 15:17,18.

Emotionally, repentance is a change in attitude and feeling. It includes a sorrow for sin *and* a desire for pardon. This element is reflected in the following verses: Psalm 51:1,2; 2 Corinthians 7:9,10; Psalm 38:18.

The change in the will that grows out of true repentance is an *inward* turning from sin. This inward element is extremely important because the outward turning from sin is a product of the transformation wrought by inner regeneration. To place it as a condition for salvation, rather than as a product of salvation is dangerously close to adding a work to salvation. This element is reflected in the Greek word *metanoia*, which means a change of mind, not a change of actions.

2. *Saving Faith.* Repentance is certainly essential in conversion, yet it doesn't constitute all of the elements of conversion. Equally important is the element of saving faith. The Scriptures abound with teachings on the necessity of saving faith:

> Therefore, since we have been justified through *faith*, we have peace with God through our Lord Jesus Christ (Rom. 5:1).

> For it is by grace you have been saved, through *faith*
> — and this is not from yourselves, it is the gift of
> God . . . (Eph. 2:8).

These are but two of many verses referring to the necessity of
faith for true conversion. The question again arises, What is
saving faith? A simple definition of saving faith is that it is a
conviction of truth involving the will, intellect, and emotions.

Intellectually, saving faith is the belief in the truth of God's
Word as it relates to the essentials of salvation. It is here that the
Holy Spirit convicts a man regarding truth. A person must believe God when he talks about sin and salvation. This is clearly
implied in Romans 10:14,17. Saving faith is faith based on *facts*;
it is not just an emotional leap into the unknown.

Emotionally, saving faith is an awaking of the soul to its
need of salvation and a desire to commit oneself to the truth of
the gospel. This element is clearly shown in Psalm 106:12 and
Matthew 13:20. Although this is a basic element of saving faith,
it is not the only one. Appeals to the emotions are communicated
more quickly than appeals to the intellect, yet they will not
produce true conversion apart from the communication of the
facts of the gospel.

In the element of the will, saving faith is a personal trust in
Christ shown by (1) trusting Christ as Savior, (2) turning from
self-controlled living (i.e., surrender of heart), and (3) determining to follow Christ obediently as Lord. This element is also
necessary as shown in John 1:12 and Revelation 3:20.

We have looked at how true conversion is a product of
repentance and saving faith. The question of how to effectively
communicate this truth still remains. The previous discussion is
obviously too deep for a new Christian. I have developed a
simple diagram for communicating this truth and it is shown in
Figure 18. As I draw out the diagram with a person involved in
follow-up, I simply explain the principles involved. Often, the
Holy Spirit uses this time to really convict him about the truth of
the gospel. Following is the diagram I use:

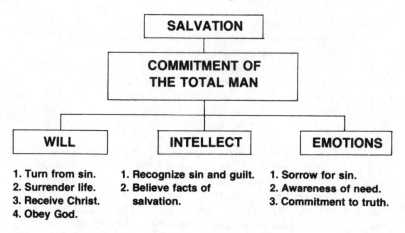

Fig. 19 Conversion Diagram

By using this diagram I can communicate the truth without using words difficult to define for a new Christian. This method has proved effective in the experience of many people.

Are there other possible reasons why a person could not receive assurance of salvation in addition to the fact that he may not be saved at all? I have found through experience several other possible causes of this condition in a new Christian. I will list them but not elaborate on them because the vast majority of cases are solved in the preceding fashion. The following is a list, with Scripture references for further study:

1. Unwillingness to make restitution (Num. 5:6,7).
2. Unwillingness to forsake a gross sin (Prov. 28:13).
3. Unrepented bitterness toward parents/family (Heb. 12:15; Eph. 6:1,2).
4. Severe counseling problems.

Problem 3: Guilt

Often in follow-up you will encounter someone who seems

101

to have a problem with guilt in his life. He has a difficult time actually experiencing forgiveness. This problem varies widely in complexity. In some cases the solution may be simple, in others it might require some competent Christian counseling. If it is one that requires counseling, I hope you have access to a good pastor-counselor in your vicinity. I am becoming increasingly convinced of the necessary role of trained, competent, biblically oriented counseling to supplement the work of personal follow-up.

The first step in dealing with this problem is to teach the new Christian what the Word of God says about confession of sin. Follow-up Appointments IV and VII deal with this topic and can be reviewed in Appendix 1. There are two points to make clear to the new Christian: Temptation isn't sin, and God promises forgiveness and cleansing. Many new Christians are suffering from false guilt caused by a misunderstanding of temptations. They often mistakenly identify the temptation as the sin. They need to be shown that temptation is not sin, that they can expect it to come, and that they can have victory over it according to 1 Corinthians 10:13. Once a person realizes this truth, the problem of guilt is often solved. A correct understanding of the totality of cleansing promised in 1 John 1:9 will do much to keep the new Christian from being overly introspective.

At times a persistent guilt problem reveals that restitution has not been made when God was leading the person to do so. Restitution not only implies the paying back of unlawful gain, but also the need for reconciliation. In your counseling with this new Christian, see if there is someone with whom God has been leading him to seek reconciliation. Matthew 18:15 implies the importance of this step for real growth in Christ. For an in-depth examination of this truth and its relationship to effective counseling of guilt see the book *Christian Counselors Manual* by Jay Adams.[2]

At times guilt is an indication of incomplete repentance on the part of the new Christian. Perhaps there has been a secret refusal on his part to forsake a particular sin. He must be shown that confession is not a gimmick, that it was not given as a way to "kiss and make-up" with the Lord, but it is a valid way of dealing with sin *only* when that sin is forsaken. Isaiah 55:7 states:

Let men cast off their wicked deeds; let them banish from their minds the very thought of doing wrong! Let them turn to the Lord that He may have mercy upon them, and to our God, for he will abundantly pardon! (Living Bible).

If guilt still remains after you have taken these steps, refer the new Christian to a competent biblical counselor. You have done as much as you are able to do. Even though I encourage this referral to counseling, keep in focus that guilt could be a deceptive device of Satan to make the new Christian doubt God's love and forgiveness. Pray that God would give you discernment in this problem.

Problem 4: Undisciplined Devotions

A consistent devotional life is one of the most important building blocks for growth in Christ. It is through this means that a Christian begins to discover what it means to be in personal daily communication with the Lord. Lack of consistent devotions is usually the cause, directly or indirectly, of much spiritual ineffectiveness. It is important that this condition not be allowed to continue for too long a time. Consistency in prayer and Bible study must be developed in the life of the new believer.

There are several reasons a person might be having problems with his devotions. First, there may be a lack of motivation to study the Bible. Perhaps the new Christian doesn't realize the need for a devotional life. He has no understanding of the role of the Word of God in true growth. He has never read 1 Peter 2:2: "Like newborn babies, crave pure spiritual milk, so that by it you may grow up in your salvation."

True motivation is a product not only of "what," but also "why." The new Christian must see "why" the Bible is so important to growth. Second Timothy 3:16,17 explains the "why's" of Bible study:

All Scripture is God-breathed and is useful for teaching, rebuking, correcting, and training in righteousness, so that the man of God may be thoroughly equipped for every good work.

103

This passage elaborates the uses of Bible study and lists them: teaching, reproof, correction, training.[3] The Bible teaches us God's will for our lives. It also reproves us when we are doing wrong. The Bible never stays on the negative, but goes on to the positive and teaches us how to correct our wrong-doings. It then goes on to show us, in a general way, what to do to insure that correction takes hold by training us in righteousness. When a new Christian begins to understand the "why" of devotions, he often needs no more encouragement to become consistent.

A second reason a person might have difficulty being consistent in his devotional life involves a lack of adequate training. In many cases, a person simply doesn't know how to have a devotional time. If this is the case, it will do little good to keep exhorting him to have one without also showing him how. Follow-up Appointment II in Appendix 1 has some practical suggestions on how to give this training to a new Christian. You will find some people who need more than just some insight into asking questions and meditating on Scriptures. For these people to become effective in Bible study, they need the additional help of a planned program of study in already-published, devotional study books.

A third reason for devotional problems arises out of a lack of discipline. The new Christian may have trouble disciplining himself to study. In this case, it will be important to discover whether this lack of discipline is only evidenced in devotions, or if it is also seen in other parts of this person's life. If it is only evident in the area of devotions, then it can usually be solved by dealing with it as a motivational problem and giving him a relatively easy devotional study book to prevent discouragement. However, if the lack of discipline is evidenced in other areas of his life, it becomes a much more difficult problem. This person has a habit of laziness. Although the new Christian often desires devotions, he is prevented from having them because of this problem. In this case, it is best to begin helping him live in a disciplined way in other areas of their life as well as in devotions. This will take a great deal more time and is much more difficult than any other problem with devotions.[4]

Problem 5: Fear in Witnessing

This particular problem is a common one. Many new Christians (perhaps many old as well) are afraid to publicly identify themselves with Christ. Most often this fear expresses itself in a fear of witnessing, because witnessing is about the only way a person publicly identifies with Christ in a country where persecution of Christians is infrequent. It is important that this problem be dealt with early in the personal follow-up of a new believer. The best way to deal with it is to find the cause of the fear and show the biblical solution.

For many new Christians, fear in witnessing is nothing more than a normal fear connected with talking to strangers. This kind of fear, especially for those suffering from shyness, is natural. Even Paul fell into this kind of fear, as described in 1 Corinthians 2:3: "I came to you in weakness and fear, and with much trembling." Many can identify with this feeling. The solution lies in merely pointing out that this is a common problem, and then showing how God can give the strength one needs to serve Him.

At times, a fear in witnessing arises out of a lack of training. Many Christians, both new and old, are simply not sure what to say about Christ. This problem is a simple one to solve. All you do is lead them into some training. There are a number of good training programs available for this purpose. Several books concerning evangelism are listed in Appendix 2.

In some cases, fear in witnessing has its roots in the fact that a person has been living an inconsistent life and others know it. This is the old hypocrisy problem, Paul was aiming at it when he commanded in Philippians 1:27: "Whatever happens, conduct yourselves in a manner worthy of the gospel of Christ." Consistency of life will clear up this problem for most people.

In some instances, people have a genuine fear of persecution for identifying with Christ. In cases like this, focus your counsel on the truth that he need not fear man when God is on his side. "The fear of man lays a snare, but he who trusts in the Lord is safe" (Prov. 29:25). God can strengthen him to face all persecution. There is never an excuse not to be identified with Christ in this world. God can always work out His perfect will, even in the midst of adverse circumstances (see 2 Timothy 2:12; Matthew 10:32,33).

Problem 6: Involved in a Weak Church

Often when you begin follow-up with a new Christian, he is already involved in a local church. Perhaps it is liberal or dead and cold, a bad environment for the babe in Christ. You are faced with the dilemma of how to move him to a new church tactfully. The first step in this transfer is to teach him the church's role in his own growth in Christ. Follow-up Appointment III in Appendix 1 deals with this teaching. Often, just understanding what God's purpose is for the church will motivate the new Christian to seek out better church fellowship.

It is also good to explore the ability the new Christian has to change churches. In the case of a youth ministry, often the parents refuse to allow their child to go to another church. It is important that you don't encourage disobedience in this situation. Involve the young person in a good Bible study or fellowship group that meets outside the church. This is not as good as involvement in the church itself, but is better than no fellowship and teaching at all.

In the case of an adult who is reluctant to change, don't push hard at first. This will tend to put him on the defensive and could affect your whole personal follow-up relationship. The whole issue of church membership is a touchy one. Your church could be labeled a "Sheep Stealer" if you are not sensitive in this area. Although I am convinced it is God's will to put a new believer in a growing, warm Christian environment, it is not always clear where this new church ought to be. Certainly it is imperative that a new believer be strongly urged to leave a cult or sect, as well as a clearly liberal church. When leaving a cult or sect, the new Christian is easily moved to your home church without incurring problems with other churches. I have found it best to move a new Christian from a liberal church to an evangelical one within his own denomination, if there is one available. Be discerning and remember, in the final analysis, the most important thing is the growth of the new Christian. If this means conflicts, then you needn't feel guilty.

Achieve the change you desire step by step. Begin by inviting the new Christian to church activities that do not conflict with regularly scheduled services at his original church. As he gets involved, it won't be long before the difference between good Christian fellowship and what he is experiencing in his own church will become evident to him. This should do much to aid him in making the transition. Don't force the issue but allow for the convicting ministry of the Holy Spirit in his life. I am assuming that the person doing the follow-up is involved in a good church. If this is not the case, then you should carefully analyze why you are attending a church to which you would not invite a new Christian.

Problem 7: Family and Peer Opposition

A problem facing some new Christians is active opposition to their new commitment by family and friends. I touched on this briefly under the problem of persecution in witnessing. Some people face extreme opposition in their closest associates. This kind of opposition often turns many away from following Christ. When this is a problem, you must begin immediately teaching the new Christian about the worth of knowing Christ. Begin to share Scriptures like the following:

> But whatever was to my profit I now consider loss for the sake of Christ. What is more, I consider everything a loss compared to the surpassing greatness of knowing Christ Jesus my Lord, for whose sake I have lost all things. I consider them rubbish, that I may gain Christ (Phil. 3:7,8).

> And everyone who has left houses or brothers or sisters or father or mother or children or fields for my sake will receive a hundred times as much and will inherit eternal life (Matt. 19:29).

When the source of this opposition is too close to the new believer, it places even greater urgency on you to establish a friendship with him and get him into fellowship with other Christian friends as well. Only then will his chances of making a break with his old friends improve. In the case of his family, he cannot sever relationships. God's command to honor and love parents was given for all time. It is only when parents seek to make a child deny his faith that he is not under obligation for obedience. If the door to the family closes, it must never be from the Christian's side. This would only hinder the gospel's chances in the hearts of the family. Stick close to a person experiencing this kind of opposition because he needs all the personal attention he can get. Pray much concerning this kind of a problem.

Problem 8: Credibility

Sometimes a person doing personal follow-up encounters a credibility gap with the person he is following up. By a credibility gap I mean the new Christian doesn't trust or believe what you tell him. This is a serious problem because the new Christian must look upon you as an authority before he can gain the proper motivation to learn and apply what you are teaching him. There is no easy answer to this problem. I have found credibility to have many facets. It is difficult enough merely to analyze why someone lacks credibility, much less tell someone else how to achieve it. In a future book on leadership development, I hope to explore in much greater detail this question of credibility. For now I would like to offer you a list of the ten most common factors people identify as reasons for credibility. This list is compiled from counseling with all age groups. I hope it will stimulate your thinking in this all-important area.

Factors Contributing to Credibility:

1. Being well organized in keeping follow-up appointments.
2. Knowing where to find answers in the Bible.
3. Being nondefensive, open.
4. Knowing clearly what you believe and why you believe it.
5. Being able to share answers out of experience, not just theory.
6. Fruitfulness in evangelism.
7. Enthusiasm in ministry.
8. Remembering what was discussed at previous appointments.
9. Consistency of life.
10. A good home and obedient children.

Problem 9: Intellectual Hang-ups

A new Christian will sometimes be exposed (through classes or discussions) to a convincing argument against some point of Christian truth. In the face of this argument, he begins to have questions and perhaps even doubts about his faith. It is important that you help him through this crucial period of his life. Don't pass over it hoping he will outgrow the questions.

The first thing to impress upon the new Christian is the ability of the Christian faith to hold up under testing. The Christian faith is not gained at the cost of intellectual suicide. It is not a "blind" leap of faith into the unknown.[5] It is a factual faith built on the revealed truth of God's Word. There are legitimate and logical answers to almost any question with which he might be confronted. This point should be clear in the mind of a new believer.

The second point to share is that the new believer's faith is never to rest on any other foundation than Christ. Although answers to questions are important, they are only to reinforce, *not* replace, the foundation of Christ. It is important to make this point clear so a new Christian will build his faith on the revealed truth of the Word of God rather than philosophical speculation, no matter how convincing it may be.

Another truth to communicate is the fact that questions in themselves are not wrong. Questions often are indications of a hungering and thirsting to know more of God's truth. Don't ever scare a new believer into not asking questions. This will seriously hinder his growth. Asking questions is not wrong. Rather, it is allowing these questions to breed doubt in our minds that makes it sin. We may question, but it should be from the standpoint of confirming where we stand and seeking a more definitive picture of our position. Make certain the new believer understands this.

The best way to answer serious questions is through suggested readings and subsequent discussion. Many excellent books on nearly all aspects of Christian apologetics have already been written. These should prove to be beneficial for your edification as well as the new believer's. Appendix 2 contains a listing of excellent apologetical books in a variety of categories.

Problem 10: Doctrinal Difficulties

Some new Christians become involved in extremes in some aspect of doctrine or Christian living. This is a serious problem and can greatly retard their growth. This problem arises because of the immaturity of a new believer. As a new Christian, he is a babe in Christ, and, like other babies, exists on the emotional level most of the time. There is little intellectual content to his faith. This makes a good breeding ground for questionable extremes.

The first step toward solution is to involve the new believer in a strong teaching situation where he will gain much solid biblical knowledge. This input will greatly help to stabilize him. Think through with him the points of legitimate differences among Christians (i.e., baptism [mode], church policy, etc.). He should see that you are not so narrow as to allow no differences of opinion. But he must see that you are unswerving concerning major doctrines that are legitimate grounds for dogmatism. The basic doctrines of the faith need defending and the truths of abundant Christian living must be guarded against extra-biblical additions. Caution him against attending meetings of groups that would fall outside the walls of solid evangelical Christianity. These things should do much to solve this problem.

CONCLUSION

We have examined a number of basic problems in this chapter. I hope you are getting a feel for some of the things you will face in a ministry of personal follow-up. The ideas expressed in this chapter are meant to stimulate your own research, not stagnate it. Because of the limitations of space, I have purposely not gone into a number of minor problems. The methods of dealing with problems explained above should give you guidelines toward developing your own solutions to the problems you will face in your personal follow-up ministry.

Notes

[1] I would recommend study on these doctrines by reading the following portions of books:

> L. Berkhof, *Systematic Theology* (Grand Rapids: Eerdmans, 1972), pp. 356-549.

> Henry Clarence Thiessen, *Introductory Lectures in Systematic Theology* (Grand Rapids: Eerdmans, 1963), pp. 312-403.

> J. Oliver Buswell, *A Systematic Theology of the Christian Religion*, Vol. II (Grand Rapids: Zondervan, 1972), pp. 1-213.

[2] Jay Adams, *Christian Counselor's Manual* (Grand Rapids: Baker, 1974), pp.52-70. This contains the most practical discussion of this topic I have found to date.

[3] Adams, *Competent to Counsel*. Dr. Adams makes a sound exposition of 2 Timothy 3:16,17 and develops a system of counseling based on its truths.

[4] See discussion of this topic in: Adams, *Christian Counselor's Manual*, pp.171-215.

[5] For a good discussion of why many people view Christianity as a "leap" of blind faith, read: Francis Schaeffer, *Escape From Reason* (Downers Grove, IL: IVP, 1968).

6

Motivational Factors in Follow-up

Having examined problem-solving as it relates to personal follow-up, we now move on to a discussion of how to motivate the new Christian to grow in Christ. Motivation is certainly one of the most important aspects of a total personal follow-up ministry. The best personal follow-up plan in the world will be doomed to failure unless the new Christian can be motivated to follow it. Motivation is essential to good leadership because we must be able to get people to follow us if we hope to be a leader in more than name only. This chapter is by no means an exhaustive study of motivation, but rather it is a discussion of factors that have become obvious to me as I have tried, and sometimes failed, to motivate new Christians to grow.

Factor 1: Pray for Them

True motivation begins by focusing on the vertical rather than the horizontal. Only God can truly motivate people to desire to grow in Christ. Through the convicting and convincing ministry of the Holy Spirit, a person receives the strongest motivation for growth. This dynamic of motivation is set off through our faithful intercession in prayer. Scripture abounds with examples of this truth.

An examination of the gospel records shows that prayer occupied a vital role in the Lord's earthly ministry. The best example available of the content of His prayer life is found in John 17, i.e., the high priestly prayer of Christ. We see specific points of motivational prayer as we find Jesus praying for the disciples' growth, sanctification, and unity. This clearly alludes to the use of prayer in stimulating individuals to grow.

Paul gives us another example of the use of prayer in motivating new Christians for growth. In Colossians 1:9 we read:

> . . . since the day we heard about you, we have not stopped praying for you and asking God to fill you with the knowledge of his will through all spiritual wisdom and understanding.

And in 1 Thessalonians 3:10 Paul says:

> Night and day we pray most earnestly that we may see you again and supply what is lacking in your faith.

One more example of this truth is found in 2 Thessalonians 1:11:

> With this in mind we constantly pray for you, that our God may count you worthy of his calling, and that by his power he may fulfill every good purpose of yours and every act prompted by your faith.

Scripture is filled with examples of the role prayer plays in motivation. One reason for this is the role of petitioning the work of the Holy Spirit. Praying also increases our burden for the new believer. I have found in my own ministry over the years that the person I prayed for consistently was the person for whom I became most burdened. Even if I weren't burdened initially, I prayed for him out of faith and obedience to God's commands. Yet, as I prayed, the burden began to develop. This burden for the individual plays a vital role in the other factors of motivation we will discuss. Prayer not only sets in motion the motivation of a new believer, but it also develops a burden for follow-up in your own life. This is why I have placed prayer at the beginning of an examination of motivational factors. Remember James

5:16: " . ... The prayer of a righteous man is powerful and effective."

Factor 2: Love Them

Love is another of the most basic motivational tools. The role of love in follow-up has already been examined as it related to other aspects of personal work. It also plays a vital role in motivation, affecting nearly every factor involved. The type of love that motivates people is a concerned, selfless love. This type of love is only available from God. Philippians 1:8-11 relates Paul's stress on the role of love in motivating true spiritual growth:

> God can testify how I long for all of you with the affection of Christ Jesus. And this is my prayer: that your love may abound more and more in knowledge and depth of insight, so that you may be able to discern what is best and may be pure and blameless until the day of Christ, filled with the fruit of righteousness that comes through Jesus Christ — to the glory and praise of God.

Notice that there are two dimensions to the type of love mentioned by Paul. First, there is the personal dimension. God must give us a love for the new Christian. That the source of this love is in God is clearly taught in such passages as Romans 5:5 and Galatians 5:22. The goal we should be striving for is to be able to truly say we "long for all of you with the affection of Christ Jesus." This type of affection is demonstrated for us in the gospel narratives of Christ's life and is described in 1 Corinthians 13:4-8. This is the *agape* love that is only available from God.

The second dimension of this love is the reciprocal love of the new Christian being returned to us. Paul prayed that "your love may abound more and more." True motivating love is best distinguished by the reflective ability it displays. Our love should be reflected and returned by the new believer. Not all people will respond to our love the same way, yet if we never see a reflected love, it would be wise to analyze our lives and see if we are perhaps at fault.

This concerned, selfless, motivating love will reveal itself in several practical ways. It will first of all prevent us from giving up too soon (or giving the impression we are) on a new Christian who is having problems. Jesus was probably often discouraged in His ministry to the twelve, yet He never gave up on them. A new Christian needs encouragement much more than discouragement. To become an effective motivator it is important in personal follow-up to develop the fruit of patience and forbearance. A child doesn't walk on the first try or without practice. In the same way, a new Christian's growth is marked with stumbling.

Secondly, concerned, selfless love will be seen through giving the new Christian the right to make mistakes. You probably made a few mistakes in your life and he needs the same freedom. I am not suggesting that you overlook mistakes, but rather, don't give up in the face of them. Learn to deal with them in love. It does little good to become angry with a new Christian. Rebuking with gentleness and firmness is the key to success. Paul expresses this truth in 1 Thessalonians 2:7: " . . . but we were gentle among you, like a mother caring for her little children."

The importance of firm correction mixed with love is also seen in 2 Timothy 2:24-26. Jesus gave His disciples the right to make mistakes, yet He always corrected them and trained them in how to prevent the recurrence of the problem. This was a demonstration of motivating love.

A third practical way to demonstrate motivating love is by getting to know another person really well. This is important for two reasons. First, you will be able to pray much more intelligently for the needs of a new believer as you get to know him better. We have already examined the necessity of prayer in motivation. Secondly, seeking to know him better proves you are honestly interested in him. This is crucial in developing a relationship with him, as we examined in chapter 3. Remember 1 John 4:19, "We love because he first loved us."

Factor 3: Being a Consistent Example

Another basic factor in motivation is consistency of life on the part of the person doing the follow-up. In chapters 2 and 3 we have already examined the importance of example as it relates to building up a new believer. So we won't elaborate more on this aspect here. In the sense of motivation, consistency of life plays a large role because of the effect of the identification process. The new believer naturally will seek to identify with you in past and present experiences. If your life is consistent, it gives real hope to a new Christian. As he faces the struggle of putting off the old nature and its practices and putting on the new nature with its practices (see Eph. 4:20-22), it is important that he have hope for change. Hope is a key to Christian growth for it gives the patience to face a prolonged struggle.[1] Hope in this case is produced because the new believer sees that you have gained victory over an action or attitude, and this gives him hope for his own victory. As the new Christian sees how mature you are and how far he needs to go, your consistency of life motivates him for the discipline he needs for change in the Christian life.

This is not what I initially expected to find in following up new believers. I thought that seeing how mature I was would tend to discourage them as they saw how far they needed to come. This obviously didn't happen. I think there are two reasons for this. First, I have never reached a level of maturity that awed people into defeat (does anyone?). Secondly, maturity actually does motivate. In my own experience, the opportunities to spend time with a real saint of the faith most motivated me to seek to mature in my own life. Remember 1 Timothy 4:15-17 and note the relationship between consistency and the end result in the lives of others:

> *Be diligent* in these matters; *give yourself wholly to them, so that everyone may see your progress. Watch your life and doctrine closely. Persevere in them, because if you do, you will save both yourself and your hearers* (italics mine).

Factor 4: Give Them Recognition

Recognition also plays a part in developing motivation for growth in the new believer's Christian life. I would like to suggest several practical ways in which you can use this tool for motivation effectively.

The Dynamics of Personal Follow-up

To begin with, take pains to consistently encourage the new Christian in his spiritual activities. For example, you should tell him when he has done a good job witnessing. Let him know you are aware of the progress he has made in his evangelistic outreach. This will be greatly appreciated by the new Christian, give him added confidence, and motivate him to even greater involvement. That confidence be gained is extremely important. My experience has taught me that a lack of confidence is a real barrier for many Christians and prevents them from getting involved in consistent evangelistic outreach.

Recognition must be two-dimensional. By this I mean that not only should you give recognition for the positive things a new Christian does, but you should confront him concerning the problem areas as well. Don't be afraid to tell him, if he needs it, that he could have done a better job giving his testimony. One word of caution at this point. Whenever you confront him negatively, add concrete advice as to how he can improve and solve his problem.

A second important way to give recognition is by being excited about what a young Christian has discovered in the Word of God, even when you already know that particular truth. This type of recognition will go a long way toward encouraging him to become consistent in his devotional life. The worst thing you can do is to respond to his discovery by saying you are glad he has finally learned that truth and you have known it for years. If you respond in this way, you will effectively squelch any motivation for Bible study in the new believer's life. He will feel that rather than spend his time studying, he should just come to you to learn everything. You can be *genuinely* excited about what the new Christian is sharing with you because it proves he is really beginning to study the Bible for himself.

A third practical way to use recognition as a motivational tool is to make sure *he* knows that *you* know what he is doing. Nothing motivates a person like the knowledge that someone knows where he is and what he is doing. This is especially true in the spiritual realm. This was the genius of the "Class Meeting" of the Wesleyan Revival in England. Each member would check up on the other to keep one another in line. It wasn't done from a carnal motivation, but rather because each member realized that it would help the other grow in Christ and thus they desired it. Paul made it a point to know what was happening in various churches, and he let the people know that he knew. His Epistles point this out to us.

One further point about recognition must be made. Recognition never implies flattery. Flattery is defined as "unwarranted or insincere praise." Flattery never edifies a new believer, but rather it gratifies his sinful vanity. Flattery is sin, and this truth is clear from Psalm 12:2,3; Proverbs 28:23 and 29:5. Flattery does not motivate except toward sin. Remember Colossians 2:5:

> For though I am absent from you in body, I am present with you in spirit and delight to see [recognition] how orderly you are and how firm your faith in Christ is.

Factor 5: Rebuke When Necessary

The negative dimension of recognition has been mentioned in the preceding discussion. I would like to examine the role of rebuke in greater detail. In follow-up you will often need to use the spiritual knife (Heb. 4:12). Rebuking a new Christian is accomplished by confronting him scripturally with the fact that his action or attitude is wrong. This confrontation is then followed by showing him the importance of repentance, forsaking, and confession. For an in-depth examination of these practices, read the *Christian Counselor's Manual* by Jay Adams.[2] To elaborate on them is beyond the scope of this book.

It is important to realize that it will be painful to rebuke the person with whom you are working. Although this confrontation will be difficult, it will produce real change in the long run. I have found that it is easy to forget about the need for discipline in Christian growth, but the Bible is clear in its commands for involvement in this work (see Romans 15:14; Colossians 3:16; 2 Thessalonians 3:16; etc.). This type of involvement, as difficult as it is, really proves you are concerned about the new believer. It proves you are willing to do even the hard things to help him grow in Christ. Hebrews 12:11 points out that "no discipline seems pleasant at the time, but painful. Later on, however, it produces a harvest of righteousness and peace for those who have been trained by it."

Factor 6: Communicate Effectively

Effective teaching and training play a vital role in motivat-

119

ing the new Christian. My purpose is not to elaborate on all that is involved in the methodology of effective education, but rather to point out some practical helps to insure a more effective, motivating, teaching ministry in your follow-up of new Christians. These points, while certainly not exhaustive, have proved important in my own discipling ministry with people of all age groups.

1. *Carefully prepare what you are going to teach.* This will be integral to the structured one-to-one phase of follow-up (see chapter 7 for a discussion of this type of work). A basic rule of preparation is to spend three hours in study and be able to present nearly twice the information you are planning to share for a thirty-minute follow-up teaching session. This will give you a great deal more confidence in your ability to answer questions that might arise.

A consistent problem that occurs during my training seminars involves dealing with questions. The follow-up appointments in Appendix 1 are written so you will know more about a certain truth than you are going to communicate. This should solve ninety percent of your problem in answering questions. Experience will solve another nine percent, and there will always be some questions you won't know how to answer. Good preparation gains you credibility with the person you are following up and the benefits of this are obvious. (See discussion of credibility in chapter 5.)

2. *Personalize your applications to the individual you are following up.* To do this effectively will require effort, but will greatly increase the probability of lasting change in a new Christian's life. It is generally easy to come up with the general truths and principles of God's Word as we study it. It becomes somewhat more difficult to make applications to one's own life. It becomes extremely difficult to make suggestions for applications in the person you are following up. Unless you are really getting to know this person well, you will not be familiar enough with his needs to personalize your teaching. James 1:22 applies here: "Do not merely listen to the word, and so deceive yourselves. Do what it says." Seek to prevent the absorption that does not apply God's Word to the new Christian. Remember Hebrews 5:11-14:

We have much to say about this, but it is hard to explain because you are slow to learn. In fact, though by this time you ought to be teachers, you need someone to teach you the elementary truths of God's Word all over again. You need milk, not solid food! Anyone who lives on milk, being still an infant, is not acquainted with the teaching about righteousness. But solid food is for the mature, who by constant use have trained themselves to distinguish good from evil.

3. Learn to discern the verbal and nonverbal feedback you receive during a follow-up appointment. To accomplish this you must be a good listener. Verbal feedback is a good clue as to how well the new Christian is understanding what you are teaching him. Is he asking clarification questions about the crucial spiritual truths you are relating? Does he seem frustrated in making applications as you have suggested? Does he betray an inability to understand some of the most basic truths of the faith? These and other clues returning to you in the form of discussion and questions should alert you to areas of ineffectiveness in your own teaching.

Nonverbal clues will give you insight into the new believer's problem areas. Such things as embarrassment, nervousness, blushing, tension, evasion, changing subjects, etc., will clearly designate problem areas for your counseling. As a result of this sensitivity, you can begin to really zero in on basic problems and misunderstandings he may have. Your ability to do this will contribute to your credibility in his eyes and will go a long way toward motivating him for real spiritual growth.

4. Give specific and workable assignments. Nothing is as frustrating, defeating, and paralyzing to a new believer as problems in assignments. This is especially true when your follow-up revolves around the giving of assignments for personal study. Giving specific assignments and writing them out for the new believer is a key way to help prevent misunderstanding in follow-up. This will be difficult because it is much easier to give general assignments. It is also important to give workable assignments. A new believer will become discouraged if he is consistently unable to complete what you have assigned him to do. Be sure to take into consideration the variables of immaturity, lack of discipline, and motivation when making follow-up assignments. Above all, be realistic.

Factor 7: Expect Results

It is important to create an atmosphere of expectation for motivation in your personal follow-up. Your attitude will go a long way toward creating this type of atmosphere. Do you really expect that the new Christian will grow and reach out and become an effective member of the kingdom of God? Your attitude will do much to motivate his growth. If you don't really expect that he will grow and become fruitful, there is a good chance he won't. Look at Paul's attitude of expectancy in Romans 15:14: "I myself am convinced, my brothers, that you yourselves are full of goodness, complete in knowledge, and competent to instruct one another."

Jesus expected that His disciples would become effective and fruitful in His service. He expected this to the point of staking the future of the church on their faithfulness. In Matthew 4:19 He said: "Follow me, and I *will* make *you* fishers of men." And in John 15:16 He points out: "You did not choose me, but I chose you to go and bear fruit — fruit that will last."

It is important to expect results in follow-up. Let this expectation move beyond attitude into action by giving responsibilities to a new believer. Give him responsibilities that will stretch him and force him to turn to God for help. I have discovered that the best policy in follow-up is to push someone as *far* and as *fast* as possible. It is better to err by giving too much responsibility to a new Christian, than to err by giving too little. Giving out responsibilities develops a teachable spirit in the new believer. Let me give you an example of why this is true.

While I was working with Campus Crusade for Christ, I discovered a training trick used by the left-wing political groups on campus. If a new person wanted to join their organization, they would test him by giving him some literature and sending him to a certain location to pass it out. What they didn't tell the new recruit was that this location happened to be a favorite hang-out of extreme right-wing student groups. Needless to say, the new member would be beaten verbally to a pulp. When he came back to the left-wing leaders, battered and beaten, he was also very teachable. After such an experience, he was much more willing to listen to what they could tell him about how to deal with the problem in the future. I often send new Christians out to become verbally beaten, so they will return with a teachable spirit. Seldom has this procedure discouraged a student, but rather it has motivated him to learn more. Train him, send him out, and expect results.

Factor 8: Be Clear on Goals

Many people begin to follow up a new believer without having a clear idea of what they are seeking to accomplish in his life. It is important to have specific goals in follow-up so you can concentrate your energies on a program to accomplish these goals. Chapter 4 elaborated at some length on this need. Goals are not straightjackets in follow-up, nor do they inhibit or quench the direction of the Holy Spirit. Rather, goals should give you more freedom in follow-up because you know where you are heading. You can discern more easily what needs to be changed at any point in time in the life of the new believer to bring him to true Christian maturity. It gives you an opportunity to be systematic in the impartation of spiritual truth to a new believer. A systematic, planned follow-up program will be much more effective in stabilizing a new Christian than one that is hit-and-miss, where fundamental truths might be inadvertently overlooked and forgotten.

Goal-setting and planning are two basics of leadership. Webster defines leadership as: "showing the way, conducting or guiding or directing the path of another." This definition of leadership implies some principles for the work of spiritual leadership in follow-up. First, it implies teaching, a part of the process of showing, conducting, guiding, and directing. Second, this definition implies that you know where someone is and where you want him to go. This is clearly a reference to goal-setting and relationship. Third, this definition implies that you know where you are and where you are going. A basic factor in setting goals for others is to have already set them for yourself

We must have clearly defined goals and be able to communicate them to others. This is the only way to insure that others will develop in the direction you feel is right. The basic question you need to answer is: "What are your goals, both personal and in follow-up?" It is crucial that your goals be biblical ones. A study of Paul's goals in follow-up might be helpful at this point. He elaborates on them in Colossians 1:28 and 29:

> We proclaim him, counseling and teaching everyone with all wisdom, so that we may present everyone perfect [mature] in Christ. [Main objective of follow-up.] To this end I labor, struggling with all the energy he so powerfully works in me.

Colossians 2:2 and 3: (Practical goals to accomplish main objective.)

> ... that they may be encouraged in heart and united in love, so that they may have the full riches of complete understanding, in order that they may know the mystery of God, namely Christ, in whom are hidden all the treasures of wisdom and knowledge.

Factor 9: Participation

Participation as a factor of motivation is so obvious I hesitate mentioning it, yet for the sake of thoroughness I will. Participation is indeed a powerful motivating tool. There are many examples of this truth in secular society. For example, in the armed forces an officer is with his men in battle and this greatly increases their motivation to fight. In business, during a particularly busy time, an executive who assists in the work will find his employees greatly motivated to work harder and longer without resistance. Examples of this abound.

Paul used participation as a basic motivating tool to get the Christians with whom he worked and ministered to do the things he felt were proper. This is touching again on example, but shows a different and very practical aspect of it. In 2 Timothy 3:10,11, when seeking to motivate Timothy to become more aggressive as a Christian, Paul stated: "You, however, know all about my teaching, my way of life, my purpose, faith, patience, love, endurance, persecutions, sufferings — what kinds of things happened to me in Antioch, Iconium and Lystra, the persecutions I endured. Yet the Lord rescued me from all of them." Philippians 4:9 also clearly shows this truth. "Whatever you have learned or received or heard from me, or seen in me — put it into practice. And the God of peace will be with you."

Do what you ask the new Christian to do. Perhaps a checklist would be helpful at this point. The following is a list of actions and attitudes that need to be true of the new Christian and also of you.

Actions	*Attitudes*
1. Witness	1. Burden for lost
2. Devotions	2. Love
3. Fellowship	3. Faith
4. Stewardship	4. Hope
5. Obedience	5. Patience
6. Etc.	6. Etc.

Factor 10: Excitement

The communication of excitement as an element of motivation is more often developed by example than by exhortation. Thus, the motivation that develops from excitement is a product of how much you personally are excited about your faith. This is an unfortunate truth, because it is difficult for many of us to be as excited as we should be. Do you feel eager to witness, to be God's ambassador, and does this communicate to others? What about studying God's Word? Do you really gain much from your study, and does it generate excitement in your own life? Do you communicate a genuine excitement about fellowship with other Christians? The list of questions goes on and on but will all lead to a single point: Are you genuine in your excitement about the Christian life?

Paul placed great importance on the role of excitement for his own ministry. In the area of fellowship and witnessing, Paul's attitude is obvious in Romans 1:11,12,15:

> I *long* to see you so that I may impart to you some spiritual gift to make you strong — that is, that you and I may be *mutually encouraged* by each other's faith.... That is why I am so *eager* to preach the gospel also to you who are at Rome.

Note also 1 Thessalonians 2:8-12, along with other Scriptures. God can develop within you a genuine excitement that is visible, and this will go a long way toward motivating a new Christian to desire to grow in Christ.

Factor 11: Be Yourself

The last factor of motivation we will examine is the importance of transparency. This simply means not trying to put up a front with people, but rather being yourself. Don't pretend to be something you are not when involved in personal follow-up. There is usually subtle pressure applied to force you to do this. For one example, perhaps you know that a certain Christian is effective in follow-up and people are impressed and drawn to his life. This knowledge begins to subtly push you to act like this other person or pretend you are living the same way. It is not always wrong to conform to another's life style, especially when he is a mature Christian. The problem arises when we seek to conform beyond the spiritual and try to change personalities and such. This will lead to much pretense and affect your follow-up effectiveness. It is important to realize that God can make your life and your personality something worth communicating and copying. There is never any reason to pretend to be something you are not.

The strongest motivation tool you have at your disposal is the testimony of a changed and changing life. Let God have His way totally in your life and use this tool to the fullest. In 1 Thessalonians 2:8 Paul says:

> We loved you so much that we were delighted to share with you not only the gospel of God but our lives as well, because you had become so dear to us.

Notes

[1] See an excellent discussion on the role of hope and change in the Christian life in: Adams, *Competent to Counsel*, pp.137-143.

[2] Adams, *Christian Counselor's Manual*, pp.103-215.

7

Tying It
All Together

A basic question that arises repeatedly in any discussion of personal follow-up involves the limitations of this type of personal ministry. This question takes a variety of forms, some of which are as follows:

> Do we treat everyone the same in our follow-up ministry?
>
> Do we take into consideration any objective criteria in evaluating how much we become involved with a new believer?
>
> How long do we work with a new believer before he is ready to stand on his own?
>
> How do we pick and choose whom to spend time with when it becomes impossible to work closely and personally with everyone?

These and other questions form the groundwork for discussion in this chapter and are a fitting conclusion to this book on personal follow-up.

The Dynamics of Personal Follow-up

Definitions

In chapter 1 we discussed the concept of multiplication, a truth whose foundational importance caused this book to be written. A portion of the chapter was given over to definitions. It will be helpful, by way of summary, to review these definitions at this time:

Follow-up: The spiritual work of grounding a new believer in the faith.

Personal Follow-up: The assuming of a one-to-one relationship by a mature believer with a new Christian for the purpose of aiding the new Christian's nurture and growth.

Disciple: A Christian who is growing in conformity to Christ, is achieving fruit in evangelism, and is working in follow-up to conserve his fruit.

Discipleship Training: The spiritual work of developing spiritual maturity and spiritual reproductiveness in the live of a Christian.

Multiplier: A disciple who is training his spiritual children to reproduce themselves.

Multiplication: Third-generation discipleship training.

To effectively discuss the answers to the questions posed at the beginning of this chapter, we must clarify some basic definition problems. Why do we emphasize the importance of definitions? To answer this I would like to propose a question to you: Is there a legitimate difference between being a disciple and being a multiplier? It is obvious that this has to be determined by the definitions of these terms. Is it possible to be a disciple and not a multiplier? What is a disciple? In addition to our previous definition, the following is a list of criteria often used to identify a disciple.

1. One who follows Jesus and witnesses in the Spirit.
2. One who keeps His commandments.
3. One who is becoming Christlike.
4. One who is a learner.

    5. One who denies self.
    6. One who is available to God.

This is certainly not an exhaustive list, but it's fairly definitive. Now I raise the question again. Can you be a disciple and not be a multiplier? Is bearing fruit always indicative of multiplication?

The point of these questions is to demonstrate that it is possible for you to be an extremely mature Christian and very fruitful in winning people to the Lord, yet not be a multiplier. This comes about because multiplication is more a question of training and method than it is a question of spiritual growth or maturity. You must be a disciple before you can be a multiplier, but there is a difference. The term *disciple* refers primarily to spiritual maturity, while the term *multiplier* means reproducing fruit. And there is a difference. I think this is why we haven't seen much multiplication in the past. It isn't because the church hasn't had committed or spiritually mature people, for every generation has had spiritual men of God, some who have been multipliers as well. But generally, we haven't seen the type of personal one-to-one working that produces third-generation discipling. So it is possible to be a disciple and not be a multiplier. The reason I am dwelling on this point is that before we can really begin to answer the basic questions at the beginning of this chapter, we must be clear on this truth. Otherwise you will not know when I am discussing a matter of method and when I am discussing a point of spirituality.

When I use the term *discipleship training* I am always implying the production of multipliers, because the definition of multiplication is third-generation discipleship training. It is important to understand, however, that a disciple does not necessarily have to be a multiplier, although he will, hopefully, become a multiplier eventually. This will result if you have consistently been focusing your attention on the goal of making him effective in working with other people.

A person can be a committed, mature Christian and not be a multiplier. A perfect example of this is Dawson Trotman, founder of the Navigators. In his book *Born to Reproduce*, he relates how he was growing in Christ, and yet he was not being really effective in the area of follow-up.[1] Dawson Trotman was a disciple in his own right, as far as following God was concerned, but he was not a multiplier until he began to consistently apply himself to become one. This is the idea I want you to see. It is possible for you to be mature in Christ yet not be effective in personal follow-up. It is also possible for you to mature in Christ and not agree with the point I am making, although I would want to hear from you if you disagree on these things. I hope the preceding discussion has helped to clear up your thinking along the lines of my basic point. If it has, we are ready to move ahead.

Levels of Discipleship Training

How long do we work with a new believer in personal follow-up? A quick answer might be to work with him as long as you can. This is indeed a quick answer, but it is also meaningless. Unless you have clear in your mind the goals and objectives of your work of personal follow-up, it will be meaningless to set a time limit on achieving them. Chapter 4 went into the question of goals in much depth, yet still left unanswered is a basic question: How far do I go personally with a new believer in achieving these goals? The answer to this question lies in seeing the distinction between basic follow-up and discipleship training. Although I often use the term follow-up in a general sense to include all the nurturing of a Christian, it is being used in a limited sense in this chapter. In its limited sense, basic follow-up is the work of grounding a new believer in his faith.

Basic follow-up should be given to everyone who responds to the message of the gospel. The time duration of basic follow-up is six to ten weeks. As we discovered in our discussion of the goals of follow-up, this implies achieving such things as:

1. Assurance of salvation.
2. Teaching on how to grow in Christ.
3. Consistent devotional life.
4. Church involvement.
5. Public confession of faith.
6. Etc.

The follow-up appointments in Appendix 1 are given to help achieve these goals. It should be obvious from the previous discussion of definitions that basic follow-up, in itself, will neither disciple or make a multiplier out of a new believer. There is another phase to the overall work of personal follow-up that achieves this goal. This is the phase of discipleship training.

Discipleship training, as we have previously discussed, implies working with a new believer to achieve maturity and spiritual reproductiveness and, hopefully, multiplication. This is a much greater task than the work of basic follow-up alone. Discipleship training also differs from basic follow-up in that it is not done with everyone. Only a few are trained in this way. The reasons for this selectivity and insights on choosing them will be given later in this chapter. The biblical support for this kind of selective training is shown in the examples of Jesus and Paul. Jesus selected a small group of men out of the many who followed him with whom to work more closely:

> One of those days Jesus went out into the hills to pray, and spent the night praying to God. When morning came, he called his disciples to him and chose twelve of them, whom he also designated apostles (Luke 6:12,13).

It seems from other portions of the Gospels that, in addition to working with the twelve, Jesus worked even more closely with three of them: Peter, James, and John.[2] We also find Paul concentrating his energy on a few men such as Timothy, Luke, Titus, etc.

The criteria for choosing whom to disciple is not usually a question of good and bad, black or white. If this were the case, it would be quite a simple choice. In reality the choice is between good and best. This kind of a choice can only be made by divine insight, hence the example of Christ's spending much time in prayer before making His choice. More will be discussed about making this choice shortly.

The need before us at this point is to examine in greater detail what we mean by discipleship training. As was already mentioned, discipleship training is training for multiplication. The idea is to put your life into another person. Progress is gauged by development through a series of levels in the process of achieving effective multiplication. The following diagram illustrates these steps.

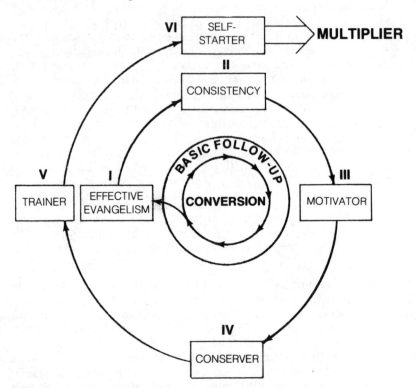

Fig. 20 Levels of Discipleship Training

Let's examine these levels in greater detail. The levels build upon one another and to a certain extent, not totally, a higher level requires the achievement of a lower level.

Level One is the achievement of effectiveness in evangelism in the life of a growing Christian. A growing believer should be achieving a fruitful outreach. This is a product of both training and experience. A number of effective evangelism training programs have been suggested elsewhere. The experience of evangelism is your responsibility. As you take a new Christian out with you and continue to expose him to witnessing involvement, this experience will grow. Unfortunately, there is no shortcut to experience.

Level Two is the achievement of consistency of growth in the life of a new Christian. This is a crucial level of development. He must become consistent in his growth to become truly effective in the Lord's work. Consistency is not the same as perfection. Consistency implies an overall direction of visible growth in a Christian's life, in spite of periodic stumbling. The question you need to answer is whether the new Christian is progressing consistently in the development of a Christlike life. Consistency is going to be achieved as a believer understands and applies the truths of Spirit-filled living, dealing with sin, obedience, trust, fellowship, and outreach.

It is important to state at this point that levels one and two are also goals of basic follow-up. You should seek these things for everyone you are in contact with in follow-up. I have included them under two areas of discipleship training to show that there is overlap between basic follow-up and discipleship training. I have also included them to show the total scope of discipleship training and the necessity of achieving some basic foundations before you can hope to begin to achieve true multiplication.

Level Three is the development of a true motivator in the person you are discipling. This is a distinct step in producing a multiplier. At this level, a Christian becomes committed enough to outreach so that both his words and life are motivating others to get involved in outreach. This is the first step up from the level of achieving the goals of basic follow-up and toward the achieving of a truly multiplying life. There is little you can do beyond example to bring a person to this level.

Level Four is the first stage of reproduction. The person you are working with is trained to work with a new Christian. He is able to go over a program of basic follow-up with a new believer and has done so successfully under your supervision. This is a distinct level of development and is the first indication of multiplication of your life in the life of another. You have trained this person through personal instruction and group training, and he has applied this training. The application of the training is an important element of this level. Obviously you cannot force application. This fact points out the truth that in discipleship training the best you can do is to provide the right environment for growth. More is "caught" than taught when it comes to disciple-building. This is in real contrast to basic follow-up where the opposite is true.

Level Five is the development of transferability in the ministry of the person with whom you are working. He gets to the point of not only following up new Christians, but he also trains other Christians to do follow-up. The other Christians may or may not be people he has led to Christ. This phase is a major one in multiplication. For the first time you are seeing not only the application of training, but also the transference of it. This level is not an easy one to achieve. As was indicated in the discussion surrounding level four, much more is caught than taught at this stage of discipleship training. This implies that a person reaches level five only after he has become consistently effective in personal follow-up of others. It is not a product of training exclusively. However, this does not imply that training is unnecessary. Quite the contrary, it is the necessity of training that led to the writing of this book.

Level Six is the final level. It is here that the stage is set for actual multiplication. Level six is the development of a self-starter. This means that the person has become totally independent of you and dependent on God. The person is faithfully reproducing your training and teaching in the lives of other people. The element of *faithfulness* is very important here. Unless the person you seek to disciple is faithful to reproduce your efforts, you have not accomplished the multiplication of your life. You, in effect, are staking your productivity in the life of the person you are discipling. If he proves unfaithful, you are frustrated in your fruitfulness. This is why Paul laid the stress on finding this type of "reliable" men as a precondition for discipleship training. Notice again 2 Timothy 2:2: "And the things you have heard me say in the presence of many witnesses entrust to *reliable* men who will also be qualified to teach others." The necessity of faithfulness is stressed in this classic verse on discipleship training and is defined, by inference, in terms of reproducing. Don't make the mistake of not fully taking this warning into consideration.

How long will it take to go through all the levels? I don't know the answer. There are so many variables in discipleship training that to setting a general rule as to time would be impossible. Later in this chapter more thought will be given to the question.

An equally pertinent question relates to methods. What do I need to know to help a person achieve real multiplication? Much of what has already been said in this book is applicable for this work, but it also requires more. Knowledge of doctrine, counseling, the Word of God, teaching technique, and more are needed to be truly effective. Let's move now to a discussion of how to pick out faithful disciples to pour your life into.

Filtering Process in Discipleship Training

Choosing individuals to pour your life into through discipleship training is one of the most critical decisions you will ever make. The outcome of your decision will determine whether you will become a multiplier. It will affect the eternal fruitfulness of your ministry in the sense of people won to Christ in the chain reaction set off by your producing of multipliers. Never go into discipleship training with an individual out of desperation or by default. Unless he is faithful, you will accomplish nothing. It is much better never to go beyond basic follow-up with someone unless he is trainable and faithful. The question before us is how to determine who is faithful and who isn't. I would like to suggest a few guidelines to follow in making this choice.

1. *Prayer.* Who to train in discipleship is such an important decision it should never be made on the basis of human wisdom alone. Prayer over this decision was the example Christ gave us in Luke 6:12,13. Although it states here only that Christ spent all night in prayer over choosing His disciples, you can be sure He spent much prior time in prayer as well. It was such a crucial decision that a mistake would have been disastrous. It is no different for your life.

2. *Insights gained in basic follow-up.* Follow-up itself has a tendency to filter out the unfaithful. Anyone who has done any personal follow-up realizes that many people start out who seem to fall by the wayside. They start missing appointments and soon they are no longer in a personal follow-up relationship with you. I have discussed in chapter 5 the way to handle this kind of problem. The point here is that often follow-up will make your choices for you.

3. *A hunger for spiritual things.* A person who expresses and displays a real hunger to grow in the Lord is usually a good prospect for discipleship training. This type of person is usually faithful in his devotions and any follow-up assignments you have given him. If this kind of hunger continues throughout the period of basic follow-up, this person could be one into whom God wants you to pour your life.

4. *A clear understanding of what has happened to him.* For a new Christian to understand what has happened in his life is a good sign. Usually this is indicative of a searching and believing heart. A person who is clear on where he stands and how he got there is apt to stay in the center of God's will.

5. *Willingness to meet, corporately and personally.* A willingness and desire for fellowship, both with you and the group, usually indicates that there indeed has been a change in the life of this person. His faithfulness in attendance at services, study times, and follow-up appointments will be an indicator of how "faithful" a man he will turn out to be.

6. *Good verbal feedback.* A person who is alert and questioning has a good potential for being a faithful trainee. You need to discern the attitude behind his questions, but usually it is a demonstration of a searching mind. If this is true it will aid him in growing in his knowledge of the Word and doctrine.

A sound evaluation of these guidelines and sensitivity to the leading of the Holy Spirit should enable you to effectively choose persons with whom to work. It could well be, at a certain point in time, that no one fits the criteria. If this is the case, don't work with just anyone, but bide your time. Do other things such as witnessing and other types of outreach until the right person comes along. Again the warning, don't disciple by default. The next point to examine pertains to the types of work you do with a new Christian after you have determined to go further with him in discipleship training.

Types of Training Relationships

A question often arises pertaining to the types of relationships you should have with a new believer. It seems obvious that your relationship with a new Christian is going to vary in terms of teaching and training as he grows. Does the amount of time spent vary over the course of personal follow-up? Does the type of relationship vary?

There are four basic types of training relationships you will have with a new believer as you go through basic follow-up and discipleship training with him. They are all types of one-to-one relationships, but the purpose and structure of each is different. The four types are as follows:

1. Relationship One-to-One.
2. Counseling One-to-One.
3. Structured One-to-One.
4. Partnership One-to-One.

Let's examine each of these more closely.

1. Relationship One-to-One. The purpose of relationship one-to-one is seen in the name. This type includes the things you do to develop a relationship with the new believer. Chapter 3 went into great depth on how to develop these relationships because a relationship must be established with a new Christian to be effective in follow-up. The content of this type of working is unstructured and not necessarily even spiritual in nature. Your object is primarily just to spend quality time with the new believer. Chapter 3 discussed ways this could be done. The following is a short summary of suggestions:

1. Sporting events
2. Dinners/desserts
3. Meetings (go together)
4. Shopping

The purpose of this type of work is to develop relationships. You are not trying to impart any spiritual insight other than the example of being a Christian in all aspects of life.

2. *Counseling One-to-One.* The purpose of this type of one-to-one involvement is character development. It is done by being with a person to detect areas that need to be dealt with to promote consistent spiritual growth. This is a difficult type of ministry, perhaps the most difficult of all. It places pressure on you to be discerning and perceptive enough to spot problems and then to have the biblical knowledge to deal with them. Counseling is not the only goal involved in this type of ministry. You are also seeking to promote consistent spiritual growth. To accomplish this you will need to discipline the person to practice those good spiritual habits that lead to consistent growth. Devotions, witnessing, prayer, Scripture memory, and such are a few of the areas requiring your disciplined involvement and teaching for lasting application to be made in the life of a new believer. This takes time. It is a kind of development achieved by meeting weekly to share together and find answers to questions and deal with problems.

3. *Structured One-to-One.* The purpose of a structured one-to-one relationship is to lay a foundation of biblical truth in a person's life. This is the type of ministry normally thought of when the word follow-up is mentioned. It involves weekly appointments with a new Christian for follow-up. Appendix 1 contains examples of such structured follow-up meetings. It is important to have this type of work, but not to the exclusion of the other types. This type phases out of your personal follow-up once the appointments are finished. You are sharing basically three foundational truths in this type of relationship:

1. Basics of doctrine
2. How-to's of growing in Christ
3. How-to's of outreach

Usually, when the personal structured one-to-one relationship is finished, it is replaced by group teaching times in the local church and Sunday school.

4. *Partnership One-to-One.* The purpose of this type of training relationship is to insure consistency of life and multiplication. This is called partnership because it occurs late in the new Christian's development through the six levels of discipleship training. This is where you have developed a person to a point of self-starting and independence, and now your relationship has the element of mutual edification involved in it. This is much less time-consuming than the other types and often can be combined with some other activity. This type of relationship is characterized by mutual prayer and study, mutual sharing, and mutual counsel. This is an unstructured type of relationship, yet necessary for continued multiplication.

There still is a question that must be answered. When, in the process of discipleship training, do you use each type of training relationship? To answer this we must first examine stages of growth in the life of a growing Christian and then relate types of relationships to stages of growth.

Stages of Growth

In the first Epistle of John we find some stages of growth in a Christian's life well marked out for us: "I write to you, dear *children*, because your sins have been forgiven on account of his name. I write to you, *fathers*, because you have known him who is from the beginning. I write to you, *young men*, because you have overcome the evil one" (1 John 2:12,13). In this passage, John clearly delineates three categories of Christian growth: children, young men, fathers. Let's look at each of these stages in more depth.

The children (or babies) are the young converts. There are two major goals during this period of a Christian's life. The first is the establishment of fellowship with God. A new Christian must learn to develop this most vital of all relationships. The second is the establishment of an active fellowship with other Christians. It is through this fellowship that a new believer receives much encouragement and protection during the time when he is weakest in the faith.

The young men are the growing, relatively young Christians. Their needs are different from the new Christian's. While the goals of the new Christian obviously must remain for the growing Christian, there are two further goals to be met. The first is a developing consistency of life, a crucial factor in becoming truly effective for the Lord. The second goal is more fruitfulness of ministry. The reasons for this are obvious.

The fathers are mature Christians who have been Christians for some time. They are in a separate category because they are the only ones able to reproduce themselves. Their needs differ accordingly. There are three major goals for Christians at this stage. The first is that there be both the acceptance and performance of a spiritual leadership role. This includes being responsible for the personal follow-up of new Christians. The second goal is the producing of multipliers. The fathers ought to be able to point someday to spiritual children, grandchildren, great-grandchildren, etc. The third goal is continued consistency of life. A father ought to be increasingly reflecting Christ in all he does.

Now the question can be answered as to what types of work to do at what stages. Because the goals of a baby Christian are fellowship with God and other Christians, you ought to concentrate on accomplishing these goals. In the beginning, a new Christian needs information more than anything else, so a structured one-to-one relationship is necessary.

The young man needs both a growing consistency of life and an effective outreach. To accomplish these goals he will need a mixture of relationships. Structured one-to-one is still needed to give more information on doctrine, apologetics, witnessing, etc. Relationship one-to-one is needed to continue to build fellowship, but the need decreases as time goes on because the relationship will develop and become solid. Counseling one-to-one is necessary because this is how he will begin to shape up the weak areas of his life. As the young man matures further, both structured one-to-one and relationship one-to-one will begin to drop off, and counseling one-to-one begins to occupy most of the relationship.

The fathers need little structured one-to-one or relationship one-to-one. The goals of this stage are met by counseling one-to-one, which later turns into partnership one-to-one. It is the mutual edification and so on that meet the needs of a mature believer.

Perhaps the following chart will help make these relationships clear. The chart also includes the levels of discipleship training as they relate to stages of growth and types of working.

RELATIONSHIP OF LEVELS, STAGES, AND TYPES
AGE IN CHRIST

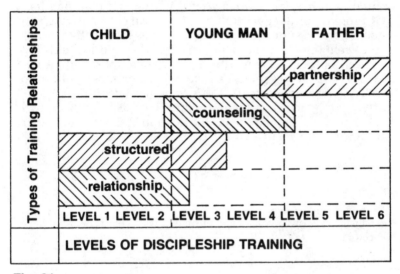

Fig. 21

How much time is involved in each type of one-to-one ministry? Although an exact answer cannot be given, certain estimates are helpful. Relationship one-to-one requires one meeting every two to three weeks until a relationship has been established. Structured one-to-one requires weekly meetings. Counseling one-to-one requires initially weekly meetings then tapers off to require a meeting only once every two or three weeks, and finally only as needed. Partnership one-to-one has no set time requirements. Thus it should be obvious that follow-up and discipleship training is extremely time-consuming in the earlier stages and then becomes less demanding as time goes by.

Conclusion

Although many subjects have been examined in this chapter, they should all contribute to your understanding this work of personal follow-up more clearly. Definitions, levels of discipleship training, types of training relationships, and stages of growth, once they begin to be understood in relationship to one another, will help crystallize your thinking and planning for a total program of personal follow-up ministry. I hope in a subsequent book to supply practical guidelines for effective leadership development in the later stages of discipleship training. However, unless one is involved in personal follow-up, it will serve no purpose to gain more training in discipleship development. It is for this reason that this book has been the first to be written. I pray that God might use it to His glory and the growth of His kingdom through the multiplication of those who prayerfully implement its truths.

Notes

[1] Trotman, *Born to Reproduce.*
[2] For a more extensive discussion of this point, see: Coleman, *Master Plan of Evangelism.*

Appendix 1

A Schedule of Ten Follow-up Appointments

PURPOSE

The purpose of this section is to provide some practical assistance for the person seeking to become involved in personal follow-up, by offering some insight into content and how to present it in basic follow-up with a new Christian. The ten follow-up appointments contained in this appendix are given as a *suggested* schedule of personal follow-up. They are a simple tool to assist the work of any Christian who is serious about personal follow-up. There are also suggested readings given to aid the development of a new believer.

The follow-up appointments are written to be personally communicated in a follow-up appointment. I have found that one-to-one follow-up is usually the most effective way of working with a new believer, but also the most demanding in the sense of knowledge. An important part of effective personal follow-up is the ability to sit down with a Bible and a blank sheet of paper and go over an important biblical truth, sketching it out for the new Christian. These follow-up appointments have been written to accomplish the above purpose. They can be given in any order deemed necessary by the person doing the follow-up, although the suggested schedule is the one most often used.

These follow-up appointments are all written in a standardized form for ease in learning. There are five divisions in each appointment.

I. OBJECTIVES: This division points out what you are trying to accomplish with a given follow-up appointment. This is important so that you will have some goal by which to measure your effectiveness.

II. REVIEW: This division gives suggestions on how to review the new Christian's progress in his spiritual growth and retention of previous teaching. Although you have already shared an important truth, there is no guarantee that it has been understood and applied by the new believer. Therefore, you must have some way of evaluating a new believer's progress.

III. LESSON: This division amplifies the teaching you are seeking to communicate on a given follow-up appointment. It gives you the necessary background information for effectively communicating the truth of a given appointment and also for answering questions that might arise.

IV. ASSIGNMENTS: This division gives some suggested assignments to aid the growth of a new believer through homework and personal study.

V. SUGGESTED PRESENTATION: This division contains a suggested way to present the main truths and Scripture references of a given appointment. It shows how to put these truths in outline form on a piece of paper for future review by the new Christian. By becoming familiar with the lesson and memorizing the one-page presentation of it, you should be able to carry on an effective personal follow-up ministry with a new Christian. This section is not meant as a straightjacket, but rather as a suggestion on presentation.

I have found that sharing the truths contained in the follow-up appointments, even when the new Christian has read about them in some book, serves to reinforce and speed application in his life. Duplication is never a problem in follow-up and actually aids in the retention of truth. The one-to-one meeting also gives the valuable opportunity to check progress and answer questions. These appointments are given to stimulate you into this all-important, and often neglected, work.

This appendix is basically to help you in the structured one-to-one relationship with a new Christian (see chapter 7). It doesn't completely cover all the things that need to be covered in this type of one-to-one ministry, yet it does present a good foundation upon which to build future teaching. I hope the format will assist you in developing appointments to cover other needy areas in the new believer's life. I trust this section will prove profitable to you.

SUGGESTED SCHEDULE OF FOLLOW-UP

Appointment I	Assurance of Salvation
Appointment II	Developing the Devotional Life
Appointment III	Church Involvement
Appointment IV	Power for Living
Appointment V	Prayer
Appointment VI	Obedient Living
Appointment VII	Dealing with Temptations
Appointment VIII	Discerning God's Guidance
Appointment IX	Developing a Testimony
Appointment X	Victorious Living

FOLLOW-UP APPOINTMENT

I

ASSURANCE OF SALVATION

I. OBJECTIVES

    A. To determine the authenticity of the new believer's commitment.

    B. To cover biblical promises essential to the gaining of assurance.

    C. To begin to develop a relationship with the new believer.

    D. To deal with any questions in the mind of the new believer.

II. REVIEW

    A. To investigate the commitment to Christ made by the new believer. Ask the following questions:

       1. Do you believe Jesus Christ died on the cross for your sins and that He rose again from the dead?

       2. Did you sincerely repent and ask Jesus Christ to come into your life?

       3. Is He in your life right now?

       4. How do you know? (Because He said He would come into my life if I asked Him to. Rev. 3:20)

    B. Review the gospel message, if necessary, by going over a gospel tract such as "Steps to Peace With God" by Billy Graham.

    C. Seek to have the new believer share what led him to make his commitment to Christ.

III. LESSON: GAINING ASSURANCE

It is important to meet with a new believer within twenty-four to forty-eight hours of his conversion. He needs to know some important truths from God's Word to keep growing in this commitment. The most important truths he needs to know are:

A Schedule of Ten Follow-up Appointments

1. Promise of Eternal Life
2. Promise of Sonship
3. Promise of Forgiven Sin
4. Need to Believe Facts, Not Just Feelings
5. Inner Witness of the Holy Spirit
6. Assurance From a Changed Life

Explain each of these points in detail to the new Christian. The suggested presentation given in Part V will give you an idea how to accomplish this.

TRUTH 1: ETERNAL LIFE

The first point to deal with is the assurance we have of eternal life with the Lord. This is a wonderful promise from God to all who believe the gospel. Encourage the new believer to think about the riches of this promise. It means not only unending life with God but also real fellowship with Him, complete fulfillment, and happiness forever. This tremendous future awaits all who respond to the gospel. The following verses would be helpful to share with the new believer:

> And this is the testimony: God has given us eternal life, and this life is in his Son. He who has the Son has life; he who does not have the Son of God does not have life. I write these things to you who believe in the name of the Son of God so that you may know that you have eternal life (1 John 5:11-13).

> For God so loved the world that he gave his one and only Son, that whoever believes in him shall not perish but have everlasting life (John 3:16).

> Whoever puts his faith in the Son has eternal life, but whoever rejects the Son will not see life, for God's wrath remains on him (John 3:36).

TRUTH 2: SONSHIP

The second truth to cover with the new Christian is the promise of sonship in the family of God. In a very real sense, we

149

become joint heirs with Christ of the promises of God. Salvation opens up a father-son relationship with God. It is important to have the new Christian realize this is a privilege and a means of assurance for him. Share the following Scriptures:

> Yet to all who received him, to those who believed in his name, he gave the right to become children of God (John 1:12).

> You are all sons of God through faith in Christ Jesus (Gal. 3:26).

> Those who are led by the Spirit of God are sons of God . . . if we are children, then we are heirs — heirs of God and heirs with Christ . . . (Rom. 8:14,17).

TRUTH 3: FORGIVEN SIN

Another major truth to communicate to the new Christian is the promise of forgiveness of sins found in Christ. This will take away the load of guilt and despair. It is an amazing truth that God loves us so much that He provided forgiveness for us. The new Christian must come to appreciate this fact. It will probably take him some time, probably weeks, to have the truth of forgiveness go beyond his head and into his heart. Work hard to accomplish this transfer. Share the following verses of Scripture with him:

> If we confess our sins, he is faithful and just and will forgive us our sins and purify us from all unrighteousness (1 John 1:9).

> This is my blood of the covenant, which is poured out for many for the forgiveness of sins (Matt. 26:28).

> When you were dead in your sins and the uncircumcision of your sinful nature, God made you alive with Christ. He forgave us all our sins (Col. 2:13).

TRUTH 4: FACTS, NOT FEELINGS

At this point emphasize the importance of believing God and taking Him at His Word. A person must learn to place his faith in the promises of God and not in what he feels. Feelings often help substantiate the truth of the Word of God, but the problem with feelings is that they are too often controlled by circumstances. Our faith was meant to rest on the solid rock of God's Word, not the shifting sands of feelings. The new Christian must focus his faith on the unchanging facts and not on the changing circumstances.

> So then, just as you received Christ Jesus as Lord (by faith), continue to live in him (Col. 2:6).

TRUTH 5: WITNESS OF THE HOLY SPIRIT

There is a legitimate place for feelings in the assurance of a new Christian. This lies in experiencing the inner witness of the Spirit of God as to his sonship. This inner witness is the sense of peace, acceptance, and forgiveness experienced in the life of the true believer. It is the sense of right standing that adds firmness to a person's commitment. It is more an inner feeling than an external emotion. The following verses clearly teach this truth:

> We know that we live in him and he in us, because he has given us of his Spirit (1 John 4:13).

> And by him we cry, "*Abba,* Father." The Spirit himself testifies with our spirit that we are God's children (Rom. 8:15,16).

TRUTH 6: CHANGED LIFE

The final point to make in seeking to give assurance to a new believer is to direct his attention to the unexplainable changes taking place in his life, both in actions and attitudes. Second Corinthians 5:17 teaches that a new Christian has become a new creation. This new creation results in a changed life and is evidenced by several things. The new Christian can use the evidence of these changes as a guideline upon which to gauge his assurance. The Word of God implies the following changes should be developing in the life of the new believer:

1. A growing hunger to know God and His Word.

   Like newborn babies, crave pure spiritual milk, so that by it you may grow up in your salvation (1 Pet. 2:2).

2. A genuine desire to keep God's commandments and have a changed life.

We can be sure we know him if we obey his commands (1 John 2:3).

3. A growing love for other Christians and desire for their fellowship.

We know that we have passed from death to life, because we love our brothers (1 John 3:14).

4. A desire to tell others about Christ.

It is written: 'I believed, therefore I have spoken with that same spirit of faith we also believe and therefore speak (2 Cor. 4:13).

For we cannot help speaking about what we have seen and heard (Acts 4:20).

IV. ASSIGNMENTS

A. Give the new Christian some good literature on beginning to grow in Christ. Following are a few suggestions to choose from:

1. Baughman, Roy. *The Abundant Life Bible Study Course.* Chicago: Moody Press, 1959.

2. Ford, Leighton. *Letters to New Christians.* Minneapolis: World Wide Publications, 1967.

3. Munger, Robert. *My Heart: Christ's Home.* Downers Grove, IL: IVP, 1954.

B. Encourage the new Christian to begin reading the Bible. If he doesn't have one, get him one. Have him start reading the Gospel of John and underlining all the promises he can find.

V. Suggested Presentation of This Appointment

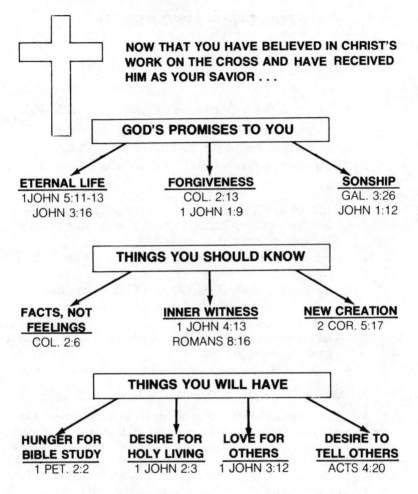

NOW THAT YOU HAVE BELIEVED IN CHRIST'S WORK ON THE CROSS AND HAVE RECEIVED HIM AS YOUR SAVIOR . . .

GOD'S PROMISES TO YOU

ETERNAL LIFE
1JOHN 5:11-13
JOHN 3:16

FORGIVENESS
COL. 2:13
1 JOHN 1:9

SONSHIP
GAL. 3:26
JOHN 1:12

THINGS YOU SHOULD KNOW

FACTS, NOT FEELINGS
COL. 2:6

INNER WITNESS
1 JOHN 4:13
ROMANS 8:16

NEW CREATION
2 COR. 5:17

THINGS YOU WILL HAVE

HUNGER FOR BIBLE STUDY
1 PET. 2:2

DESIRE FOR HOLY LIVING
1 JOHN 2:3

LOVE FOR OTHERS
1 JOHN 3:12

DESIRE TO TELL OTHERS
ACTS 4:20

FOLLOW-UP APPOINTMENT

II

DEVELOPING THE DEVOTIONAL LIFE

I. OBJECTIVES

    A. To show the importance of a time alone with God.

    B. To give suggestions for developing this time.

    C. To teach a devotional method of Bible study.

    D. To practice this method with the new believer.

II. REVIEW

    A. Investigate the amount of assurance the new believer has been experiencing. It might be helpful to review the role of feelings in assurance.

    B. Find out how much he has read of the literature you gave him.

    C. Review his study of the Gospel of John. Have him point out to you promises he has found.

    D. Get him to share with you the kind of response he is receiving from his family and friends. He might need some encouragement.

    E. Answer, if possible, any other questions he might have.

III. LESSON: DEVELOPING THE DEVOTIONAL LIFE

It is important that the new believer establish a time alone daily with God. This time is a basic part of developing a consistent walk with God. It is in these moments of intimate communion with God that we as Christians learn the most about God, His will for our lives, His guidance, and His nature. Men of God agree that this daily time of devotions is the most vital part of their day. The Word of God implies in several places the need for a time with God and His Word.

> I rise before dawn and cry for help; I hope in thy words. My eyes are awake before the watches of the

night that I may meditate upon thy promises (Ps. 119:147,148).

But his delight is in the law of the Lord, and on his law he meditates day and night. (Ps. 1:2).

Like newborn babies, crave pure spiritual milk, so that by it you may grow up in your salvation (1 Pet. 2:2).

There are a number of things that contribute to an effective and consistent time alone with God. Let's turn our attention to them right now.

PLAN FOR IT

Impress upon the new believer the necessity of planning for his devotional time. Proper planning will prevent many problems such as distractions, interruptions, and conflicts. One's devotions should be at a time when he can give his undivided attention to the Lord. Some have found that the early morning is best for them; others prefer late at night. There is no right or wrong time for devotions. The important thing is to set up a time when you are alert and can think clearly. Set up twenty to thirty minutes as an initial goal for the devotions of the new believer. As time goes on, he will probably discover he needs even more time.

FIND A GOOD PLACE

The new Christian must find a place to have devotions free from interruptions and distractions. This is important if one is to fully concentrate on the Word of God. If possible, encourage the new Christian to find a place where he can pray out loud. Sometimes it is necessary to have two places, one for study and another for prayer. In Mark 1:35 Jesus left us an example of the importance of a quiet place: "Very early in the morning, while it was still dark, Jesus got up, left the house and went off to a solitary place, where he prayed."

PROCEDURE

The new Christian needs some training on what he should do during his devotions. There are many different devotional booklets available. I have found the best way for most new Christians is not to use booklets, but rather to have an independent study program. Study the Bible a chapter or a paragraph at a time. Read the given passage slowly several times and think about the text. Here are some basic questions the new Christian could ask:

1. Does this teach me about any sins I should forsake?
2. Are there promises to claim?
3. Are there examples to follow?
4. Are there warnings to consider?
5. What does it teach me about the Father, Son, or Holy Spirit?
6. Are there any other truths?
7. What should I do about these things?

These basic questions should do much to lead the new believer into the truths of the Word. He should not only think about these questions, but also write out his thoughts. This brings us to the importance of a notebook. The new Christian should be keeping track of his daily study. This could easily be done with the aid of an inexpensive spiral notebook, approximately three inches by five inches. Set it up for each day's devotions as shown below.

As the new Christian begins to keep this notebook, it will accomplish a number of things. He will be able to check his progress and faithfulness by an objective means. It will serve to discipline his study. It will insure a higher level of learning in the new believer's life because writing underscores learning.

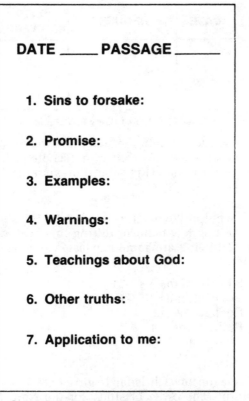

DATE _____ PASSAGE _____

1. Sins to forsake:

2. Promise:

3. Examples:

4. Warnings:

5. Teachings about God:

6. Other truths:

7. Application to me:

SAMPLE FORMAT FOR DEVOTIONAL NOTEBOOK

PRAYER

A second vital element in the devotional life of the new believer is prayer. It is important that prayer become a natural part of his life. At least five minutes of his devotional time should be spend in prayer. As time goes by, he will increase this time greatly, but to begin with, this amount of time should not prove discouraging for the new believer. Developing a prayer list is a helpful tool to aid the prayer time of the new believer. It could be kept in the back of the devotional notebook. The following format is an excellent way to develop the prayer list:

DATE	REQUEST	DATE ANSWERED

SAMPLE FORMAT FOR PRAYER LIST

A good way to get both the study and the prayer started in the life of a new believer is to buy him the notebook, set it up for him, and give it to him. This should prevent confusion.

PRACTICE

It will be helpful to practice the devotional method of study together with the new believer during this follow-up appointment. The following are some suggested practice passages to choose from:

> 2 Corinthians 5:16-21
> 1 Corinthians 13:1-7
> Romans 12:9-21
> Philippians 4:4-13
> Colossians 3:5-17

IV. ASSIGNMENTS

    A. Have the new Christian begin a notebook of devotional study. The order of study for the New Testament is optional. The following is a suggested order for the first several books.

        1. John
        2. Philippians
        3. Mark
        4. 1 John
        5. Romans
        6. Acts
        7. 1 Corinthians

    B. Have him continue reading assigned literature from Follow-up Appointment I.

V. SUGGESTED PRESENTATION OF THIS APPOINTMENT

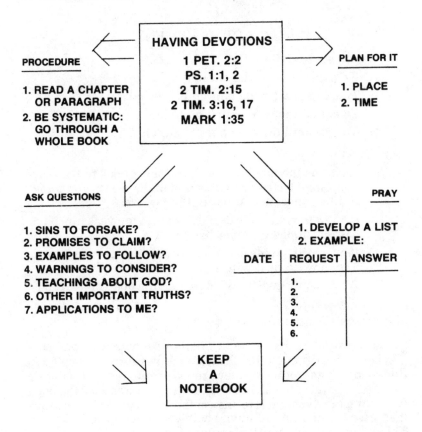

FOLLOW-UP APPOINTMENT

III

CHURCH INVOLVEMENT

I. OBJECTIVES

    A. To explain what the church is.

    B. To explain why the church is needed.

    C. To explain why we must go to church.

    D. To explain how to choose a church.

II. REVIEW

    A. Examine the notebook of devotions. Check to see how consistent he has been. Ask him to share with you some of the things he learned in the last week.

    B. Review the importance of daily prayer and ask him if he has developed a prayer list yet.

    C. If he is still having assurance problems, review chapter 5 on how to deal with it.

    D. Answer any questions before moving on to more teaching.

III. LESSON: CHURCH INVOLVEMENT

It is essential that a new Christian become involved in a good church. Although the Christian fellowship experienced in Bible studies and other similar groups is important, it is not a substitute for the church. The best way to communicate the need for church involvement is to answer the most common questions that arise in the mind of a new believer concerning a church. This is the way this particular appointment is organized.

WHAT IS THE CHURCH?

The word *church* is used in two senses in the Bible. At times it refers to the entire body of Christians in the world, i.e., the universal church. At other times it refers to a specific group of believers in a specific place, i.e., the local church. The church is often called the "body of Christ." This means that all Christians are part of the spiritual body of Christ as it ministers in our world today. First Corinthians 12:1-27 explains this important truth and shows that everyone is needed to make the body grow and become effective. A new Christian becomes a part of the body of Christ by being baptized in the Holy Spirit, which happened when he received Christ. At that time, whether he knows it or not, he became part of the body.

WHY IS THE CHURCH NECESSARY?

The church is needed for a number of reasons. The best way to communicate these is simply to list them.

1. *It is needed for the organization of believers.* Our God is not a God of disorder (1 Cor. 14:33), and it stands to reason that confusion is out of His will. Organization of believers is necessary to prevent confusion. It also provides leadership and augments growth. The need for organization is evident in Acts 6.

2. *It provides proper fellowship for believers.* Fellowship of believers is a command from God. "Let us not give up meeting together . . ." (Heb. 10:25). It is extremely important that new Christians (all Christians) have good fellowship. The church provides this. In good fellowship, believers receive mutual encouragement (Rom. 1:12), mutual edification (1 Cor. 12:14-27), and finally there is a sharing of joys and burdens (Gal. 6:2).

3. *It provides for the teaching of believers.* A good church provides needed training and teaching so Christians can grow in their own spiritual lives and minister to others. It is important to know doctrine.

4. *It gives us opportunity for group worship of God.* God desires and demands our faithful, loving worship. This worship is to be both personal and corporate. Group worship, singing, and praise is both honoring to God and helpful to our growth.

5. *It gives us an opportunity for service.* The church provides us with a place where we can use the gifts God has given us. We can work corporately toward some project or outreach. We are commanded to do works that reflect our faith.

Why Should I Go?

This is a valid question. The answer is twofold. First, you should go because of all the reasons given for why the church is necessary. Secondly, even if you didn't know all the reasons the church is necessary, it would be enough to know that God commands you to go (Heb. 10:25). In sharing this with the new Christian, it might be helpful to go even deeper in answer to this question. Group involvement tends to keep us from extremes. It is easy for the new Christian to fall into extremes in doctrine, worship, actions, and attitudes. The dynamics of a group help to check these tendencies. Also, in the church we have the benefit of mature believers who are better able to discern the answers to problems than a new Christian.

> But solid food is for the mature, who by constant use have trained themselves to distinguish good from evil (Heb. 5:14).

Which Church Should I Attend?

The new believer needs to be involved, not only in a church, but in the *right* one. There are a number of criteria that are helpful in making a choice about which church to attend. These are as follows:

1. Go to a church that preaches the gospel and has a warm, friendly atmosphere.
2. Go to a church where there is an emphasis on personal decision to receive Christ as Lord and Savior.
3. Go to a church where the members seem to understand and experience new life in Christ.
4. Go to a church where missions are emphasized and supported.

In many cases it will be helpful if you give the new believer guidance in the choosing of a church. This appointment will explain to him why you are suggesting he attend a certain church.

IV. ASSIGNMENTS

   A. Have the new Christian continue his notebook of devotional study.

   B. Make sure that he attends church this week. Give him a ride if necessary.

   C. Begin to involve him, if possible, in a home Bible study. This will serve to broaden the relationships the new Christian needs.

   D. Give the new believer some books to broaden his knowledge of the faith. Following are some suggestions:

      1. Briscoe, Stuart. *Getting Into God.* Grand Rapids: Zondervan, 1975.

      2. Ridenour, Fritz. *How to Be a Christian Without Being Religious.* Glendale, CA: Regal, 1967.

      3. Rinker, Rosalind. *The Open Heart.* Grand Rapids: Zondervan, 1969.

      4. Stott, John. *Basic Christianity,* Grand Rapids: Eerdmans, 1958.

V. Suggested Presentation of This Appointment

. . . GOING TO CHURCH . . .

A. WHAT IS THE CHURCH?
1. BODY OF CHRIST
1 Cor. 12:1-27

2.

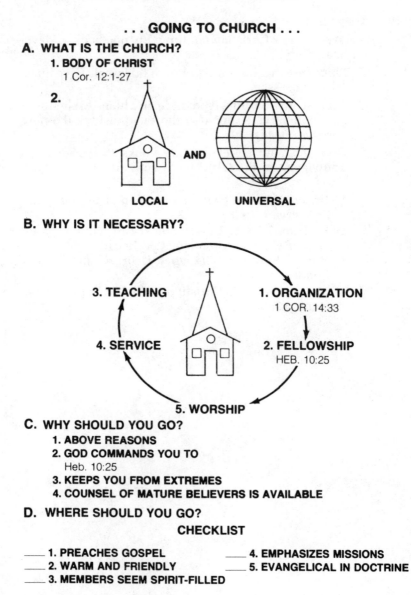

LOCAL   AND   UNIVERSAL

B. WHY IS IT NECESSARY?

3. TEACHING

4. SERVICE

1. ORGANIZATION
1 COR. 14:33

2. FELLOWSHIP
HEB. 10:25

5. WORSHIP

C. WHY SHOULD YOU GO?
1. ABOVE REASONS
2. GOD COMMANDS YOU TO
Heb. 10:25
3. KEEPS YOU FROM EXTREMES
4. COUNSEL OF MATURE BELIEVERS IS AVAILABLE

D. WHERE SHOULD YOU GO?

CHECKLIST

___ **1. PREACHES GOSPEL**   ___ **4. EMPHASIZES MISSIONS**
___ **2. WARM AND FRIENDLY**   ___ **5. EVANGELICAL IN DOCTRINE**
___ **3. MEMBERS SEEM SPIRIT-FILLED**

FOLLOW-UP APPOINTMENT
IV
POWER FOR LIVING

I. OBJECTIVES

   A. To show the promises of God relating to abundant Christian living.

   B. To show the role of the Holy Spirit in the Christian life.

   C. To explain the meaning of the filling of the Holy Spirit.

   D. To show the conditions for power for living.

II. REVIEW

   A. Examine the new Christian's notebook of devotions. Check out his consistency.

   B. Review the teaching on the church from your last appointment. Check out his commitment to church involvement. Stress again why it is important for him to be involved.

   C. Answer any other questions he might have at this point.

III. LESSON: POWER FOR LIVING

It is important for the new Christian to realize the source of power he has for living the Christian life. The significant truths of the Spirit-filled life are basic to effective Christian living. A grasp of these truths early in one's Christian experience will prevent much defeat and frustration as he grows. Today's lesson deals with this truth and follows a three-point outline that should aid retention in the new believer's life.

PROMISE AND SOURCE OF POWER

Learning to be filled, which means controlled and empowered by God's Holy Spirit, is the key to spiritual victory and effectiveness for the Christian. It is only when this condition is present in the experience of a Christian that many of the promises in the Word of God begin to become real to a Christian. Christ promised an abundant and meaningful life for His followers: "I have come that they may have life, and have it to the full" (John 10:10b).

This kind of abundant life was to be characterized by both effectiveness in ministry (service) and in personal completeness of life. Personal completeness is described by the characteristics of the fruit of the Spirit. The following verses illustrate these truths:

> You did not choose me, but I chose you to go and bear fruit — fruit that will last (John 15:16a).

> But the fruit of the Spirit is love, joy, peace, patience, kindness, goodness, faithfulness, gentleness and self-control . . . (Gal. 5:22,23).

The Holy Spirit is the source of power for this kind of Christian living. It is only when one is filled with God's Holy Spirit that this kind of life becomes possible.

> But you will receive power when the Holy Spirit comes on you (Acts 1:8a).

WHAT DOES IT MEAN TO BE FILLED WITH THE HOLY SPIRIT?

Jesus Christ lives His life in and through us in the power of the Holy Spirit. To be filled with the Spirit in a very real sense means to be filled with Christ and be abiding in Him. This is the point Paul sought to make in Galatians 2:20: "I have been crucified with Christ and I no longer live, but Christ lives in me."

The filling of the Holy Spirit is described for us in Ephesians 5:18. This passage gives us many insights into this all-important truth. "Do not get drunk on wine, which leads to debauchery. Instead, be filled with the Spirit." Here Paul compares being filled with the Holy Spirit to drunkenness. This shows that the filling is basically a matter of control. The question to ask is: Who or what is controlling you? A person who is drunk is controlled by the alcohol in his bloodstream. He is no longer behaving normally or with self-control. The person filled with the Spirit is controlled by Christ and is also not behaving "normally." Either way the person is no longer living a life controlled by self.

Being filled with the Holy Spirit is not a question of maturity as much as it is a question of control. A mature Christian will be filled with the Holy Spirit, but there are other factors contributing to his maturity. A spiritual Christian is one who is allowing Christ to control his life. He may be at one of several maturity levels, yet filled. Maturity in Christ is a product of both time and a Christ-controlled life. This is how the filling of the Spirit relates to growth and maturity.

HOW CAN I BE CONSISTENTLY FILLED WITH GOD'S HOLY SPIRIT?

There are certain conditions which must be met before one can be filled with God's Holy Spirit. These conditions are ones that need to be met continuously, not just once, because the filling of the Spirit is not a once-and-for-all act, but a continuing process. It will be important to stress these points with the new Christian. Being filled is not the product of asking, as much as it is a product of meeting the conditions.

Condition 1: Desire. A person must really want God to control his life. He must really desire the power for victorious living. The whole man — mind, will, and emotions — must be committed to Christ.

> Blessed are those who hunger and thirst for righteousness, for they will be filled (Matt. 5:6).

Condition 2: Surrender of Control. A person must make the basic decision to step down from controlling his life. No amount of wishing or asking to be filled will avail if he has not done this. He must let Christ control his life and have the use of it, before he can be filled with the Spirit. Remember Paul's attitude expressed in Galatians 2:20:

> I have been crucified with Christ and I no longer live, but Christ lives in me. . . .

This truth is also seen in Romans 12:1:

> . . . I urge you, brothers, in view of God's mercy, to offer yourselves as living sacrifices. . . .

Condition 3: Obedient Living. It is extremely important that we are walking in obedience to God's direction. A Christian has no choice but to follow God's commands as seen in His Word.

Our commitment to the lordship of Christ implies a commitment of our will to be obedient to Him in all things. Our obedience is proof of our love and our salvation. The following verses make this clear:

> We can be sure we know him *if* we obey his commands (1 John 2:3).
>
> You are my friends if you do what I command (John 15:14).

Condition 4: Cleansing. God will not fill an unclean vessel. When one sins as a Christian, he must learn to confess it to God. This is the way God has ordained for dealing with sin in our lives. This is seen in 1 John 1:9:

> If we confess our sins, he is faithful and just and will forgive us our sins and purify us from all unrighteousness.

Confession is not merely a matter of telling the Lord you are sorry for sinning, but it also includes repenting (turning from sin) and trusting God for forgiveness. These elements are essential. The word *confess* means to agree with God concerning your sin. These are the conditions for the filling of God's Holy Spirit. If you have met these conditions, then as a simple act of faith, surrender your life, ask Christ to control your life, and trust Him that He has and will continue to do so. Consistently walking in the Spirit is a product of meeting the conditions day by day. Other factors affecting maturity will be discussed in later appointments. The key truth to emphasize at this point is the importance of surrendering control of the life to Jesus.

IV. ASSIGNMENTS

    A. Have the new Christian continue his notebook of devotional study.

    B. Check up on his church involvement.

    C. Have him read one of the following books:

        1. Nee, Watchman. *The Normal Christian Life.* Fort Washington, PA: Christian Literature Crusade, 1961.

2. Ridenour, Fritz. *How to Be a Christian Without Being Religious.* Glendale, CA: Regal, 1967.

3. Schaeffer, Francis. *True Spirituality.* Wheaton, IL: Tyndale, 1971.

4. Smith, Hannah. *Christian's Secret of a Happy Life.* Old Tappan, NJ: Revell, 1942.

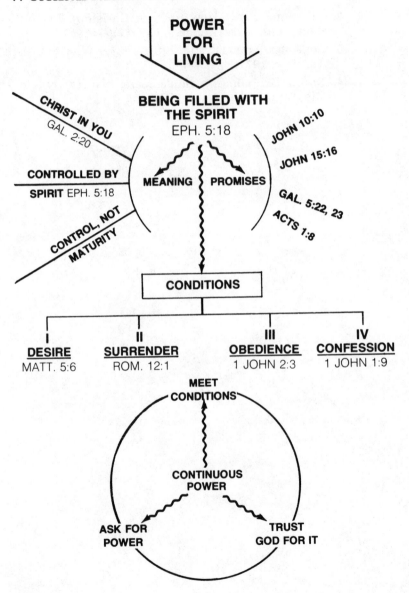

FOLLOW-UP APPOINTMENT
V

DEVELOPING THE PRAYER LIFE

I. Objectives

    A. To impress upon the new Christian the importance of developing a consistent prayer life.

    B. To show the purpose of prayer.

    C. To show how to develop an effective prayer life.

    D. To warn against possible hindrances to effective prayer.

II. Review

    A. Examine his notebook of devotions. Review with him what he is learning from his devotions. Be sure to check out his consistency.

    B. Review the previous appointment. It is important that the new Christian understands clearly what is involved in victorious living. Review by asking the following questions:

        1. Where is the source of power for effective Christian living?

        2. What does it mean to be "filled" with the Spirit?

        3. What are the conditions for filling?

        4. What does confession mean, and why is it important?

    C. Answer any questions he might have before moving into the lesson.

III. Lesson: Developing the Prayer Life

Prayer is a basic ingredient in abundant Christian living. It will be impossible for the new Christian to grow significantly in his relationship with Christ if this important element is missing. Although you discussed the setting up of a prayer list in

Follow-up Appointment II, much more needs to be taught on the topic of prayer.

Stress with the new Christian that prayer is verbal communication with God. This means that prayer is simply talking with God. It is the means God has established to enable us to respond and communicate with Him. In a sense, it is the second part of the divine communication process. The first part is God speaking to us through His Word and His Spirit. The second part is our response to Him in prayer.

Prayer is often misunderstood by the new Christian. He usually conceives of it as something dependent upon the right liturgy, terminology, or ritual. It is important to show him that prayer is simply a matter of talking with God. We don't need to know any fancy or complicated terminology or ritual. God desires us simply to talk to Him. But prayer is not just a matter of saying words. The words must be an expression of our heart. We must not only talk to God, but also mean what we say. Prayer not backed up by the heart is useless and merely an empty, meaningless procedure.

PURPOSES OF PRAYER

God's Word reveals to us a number of purposes for prayer. It is necessary to communicate these to the new Christian to achieve proper motivation on his part for involvement in prayer. The following is a list of the major purposes of prayer.

1. *Prayer satisfies the deepest needs of the human heart.* God has made us in such a way that we need the fellowship with God which is possible only through prayer. Prayer alone meets the deep, inner loneliness, and restlessness of the human heart. This is clearly taught in the following Scriptures: Psalms 42:1,2; 63:1, 5-8.

2. *Prayer is a means of discovering God's guidance.* God has determined that prayer is one of the necessary ingredients in discovering His will for our lives. The peace and direction God gives us through our prayer life is attainable no other way. Share the following verses to clearly communicate this truth: Matthew 7:7; James 1:5.

3. *Prayer is the means God has given us to deal with worry.* Worry and anxiety ought to be a foreign experience to the Christian. Freedom from these problems is a mark of the supernatural change that comes about in a Christian's life. The natural man has no way of dealing with these problems. The following verses clearly show this truth: Philippians 4:6,7; 1 Peter 5:7.

4. *Prayer is the means of communicating our needs and concerns to God.* We don't need merely to hope God knows our needs. Through prayer, God has given us a legitimate means of communicating these needs. It is also a vehicle for doing something constructive about the various things that concern us. These concerns could be people, projects, missions, etc. The following verses teach this truth: John 16:23-27; Hebrews 4:16; 1 John 5:14.

5. *Prayer aids us in our fight against sin and temptation.* One effective way to deal with sin and temptation in the Christian life is through prayer. Praying for strength and wisdom to fight temptation and win victory over sin is clearly revealed in Scripture as an important purpose for prayer. The following verses clearly teach this truth: Matthew 6:13; 26:41; 2 Thessalonians 3:1-3.

DEVELOPING EFFECTIVENESS IN PRAYER

It is not only important to know "why" one should pray, but the new Christian should have some workable suggestions on "how" to pray. The purpose of this section is to give some practical insight into developing effectiveness in prayer. The following is a list of five steps to an effective prayer life. It is important that the new Christian be clear on all of these points.

1. *Be well rounded.* A common problem for new Christians is to become extreme in one type of prayer. For example, one might continually ask God to supply personal needs; or perhaps he prays only for missions; or he might even pray for others to the exclusion of his own needs. There should be a good balance in one's prayer life. Philippians 4:6,7 relates three essential elements of effective prayer. They are as follows:

    a. Personal requests — the personal needs and desires we express to God.

    b. Supplications — the requests we make for other people and projects.

    c. Thanksgiving — remembering to thank God for His answers and provisions for our needs.

Help the new Christian to gain a balance of these elements in his prayer life.

2. *Be systematic.* Another common problem for Christians is this: They intend to pray for something and then forget about it. The answer to this problem is the development of a systematic prayer life. The best way to be systematic is to use a prayer list. Review the development of a prayer list as it was taught in Follow-up Appointment II. The following verses relate to the need of being systematic in prayer: Ephesians 1:16; Colossians 1:9; 1 Thessalonians 1:2.

3. *Be constant.* It is not only important to be systematic in praying for requests, but it is also important to be consistent in prayer in general. It is only when the new Christian disciplines himself to be consistent in prayer that he will gain the benefits of prayer. Prayer must develop into a vital and constant communication with God. A helpful way for this to occur is to develop the habit of sentence prayer. This means praying short prayers throughout the day as requests come to mind. This will, indeed, develop consistency (Rom. 12:12; 1 Thess. 5:16).

4. *Be specific.* A common mistake of many new Christians is to be too general in prayer. It is important that they be shown the need to pray specifically, for it is only this type of prayer which the new Christian will clearly see being answered. Give him suggestions on specific things to pray for.

5. *Be persistent.* Many Christians often pray once for something and no more, or they become discouraged and stop praying for something after just a short time. Although the problem of unanswered prayer is sometimes connected with praying just for things, it is also clear from Scripture that God often delays

answers to prayer at times. There are many reasons for this, but one important one is that God desires us to be patient and persistent in our prayers. It demonstrates our willingness to trust God and His timing in answers. Help the new Christian understand this truth by showing him the following Scriptures: Luke 11:5; 18:1; Romans 1:9,10.

POSSIBLE HINDRANCES TO EFFECTIVE PRAYER

A last truth to communicate to the new Christian about prayer involves the detecting of possible hindrances. The Bible discusses a number of obstacles to prayer and warns against them. The following is a list of some of these obstructions. Little comment is needed on these problems.

1. He is not praying in faith or believing (James 1: 5-8).
2. He is simply not praying enough or really asking for anything (Matt. 21:22; James 4:3).
3. He is asking for the wrong reasons (i.e., selfishness) (James 4:3).
4. He has unconfessed sin in his life (Ps. 66:18).
5. He is having unsolved marital problems (1 Pet. 3:7).
6. He is living outside God's will (1 John 5:14,15).

IV. ASSIGNMENTS

A. Have the new Christian continue his notebook of devotional study.
B. Try to set up a time just to pray with the new believer, or get him involved in a prayer group.
C. Have him read one of the following books:
1. Bisagno, John. *The Power of Positive Praying.* Grand Rapids: Zondervan, 1973.
2. Rinker, Rosalind. *Prayer: Conversing With God.* Grand Rapids: Zondervan, 1974.

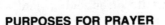

LEARNING TO PRAY
PHIL. 4:6, 7

PURPOSES FOR PRAYER

1. Satisfies Inner Needs
2. Guidance
3. Deal with Worry
4. Converse with God
5. Defeat Sin

INCREASING YOUR EFFECTIVENESS

1. Be Well Rounded
2. Be Systematic
3. Be Constant
4. Be Specific
5. Be Persistent

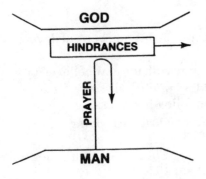

1. **NOT PRAYING IN FAITH**
   JAMES 1:5-8
2. **NOT ASKING**
   MATT. 21:22
3. **ASKING FOR WRONG REASONS**
   JAMES 4:3
4. **UNCONFESSED SIN**
   PS. 66:18
5. **MARITAL PROBLEMS**
   1 PET. 3:7
6. **REQUEST NOT IN GOD'S WILL**
   1 JOHN 5:14, 15

FOLLOW-UP APPOINTMENT
VI

OBEDIENT LIVING

I. OBJECTIVES

    A. To explain the meaning of true obedience.

    B. To motivate obedience.

    C. To give practical guidelines for becoming obedient.

    D. To suggest areas requiring obedience in the new believer.

II. REVIEW

    A. Review his notebook of devotional study. Check on consistency.

    B. Review the previous appointment on prayer by asking the following questions:

       1. What is prayer?

       2. Why is prayer necessary?

       3. How can our prayer life become more effective?

       4. What are some possible hindrances to effective prayer in our lives?

    C. Answer any questions the new believer might have.

III. LESSON: OBEDIENT LIVING

> "We can be sure we know him if we
> obey his commands. The man who says,
> 'I know him, but does not do what
> he commands is a liar, and the truth is
> not in him" (1 John 2:3,4).

Obedience is a key element in victorious Christian living. The Word of God places great stress on this expression of your commitment. In the passage quoted above, John places obedience as a sign of whether a person is truly saved. It is important that you help the new believer develop a life style of obedient

Christian living. This will not happen overnight, yet you can begin the process by making the need and method of obedience practical and clear.

What Is Meant by Obedience?

Webster defines obedience as the "state or act of being submissive to the will of another." This definition has some practical implications for the Christian. First, it implies that to be obedient, you must have some external authority as the object of your obedience. In this case, God is the authority to whom we direct our obedience. Secondly, this definition implies that true obedience is not only an act, but also an inner attitude of submission. This means that true obedience is the product of an inward determination to be submissive, not being submissive against our will.

This seems to show clearly that true obedience in the spiritual realm is the act of following God's will for our lives in all respects out of desire from the heart. True obedience to God could be defined also in terms of what it does not mean.

1. True obedience is not serving God on our own terms. Too often this is the way we seek to serve God.

2. True obedience to God will not be a product of, or result in, asceticism. We don't need to abase ourselves to be obedient to God. Obedience doesn't imply giving up fun or possessions.

3. True obedience to God is not simply outward conformity to His commandments. An important characteristic of true obedience is that it comes from the heart. If there is not a heartfelt desire to become obedient, our outward following of God's commandments becomes nothing more than legalism.

Why Should We Be Obedient?

It will be helpful to answer the "why" of obedience to properly motivate the new Christian to become obedient in his everyday life. The following is a list of three basic reasons for obedience and should be enough to motivate any new Christian.

1. *We should be obedient because God loves us and is*

worthy of our love and obedience in return. It doesn't take much meditation on what God has done for us to be overwhelmed by His unconditional love. It isn't hard to obey someone who really loves us. Examine the following verses: 1 John 4:16; 5:2; Revelation 4:11.

2. *We should be obedient because it is a practical way to prove our love for God.* This moves our love from mere lip service to actual demonstration. This proof of our love for God should be present in every aspect of our lives. The following verses make this clear: John 14:21; 1 John 5:3.

3. *We should be obedient because God clearly commands us to be.* When God commands something, we really have no option but to follow it. The following verses present God's will in this matter: Deuteronomy 10:12,13; 1 Timothy 6:14; James 1:22; 1 John 5:2,3.

How Do We Become Obedient?

It is important to give the new Christian practical suggestions on developing an obedient life. The following are four steps to achieving an obedient life.

Step 1: Know God's commands. It will be difficult to be obedient if a person doesn't know what to be obedient about. It is important to have a growing knowledge of God's Word to see clearly what God desires for you to do. God has already shown us many things about His will. The following verses comment on this: Psalm 119:11,105,130; 2 Timothy 3:16,17.

Step 2: Look to God for power. It is impossible to become obedient to God in all things on our own power. We must look to God for strength to accomplish His will. God strengthens us through His Holy Spirit. Follow-up Appointment IV dealt with how to receive God's power by being filled with the Holy Spirit. Review these truths and also share the following verses: Acts 1:8; Galatians 2:20; Ephesians 5:18; Philippians 4:13.

Step 3: Develop the right attitudes. Our attitudes toward serving God and being obedient will do much to help us or hinder us in developing an obedient life. The Word of God lists several attitudes we can be developing which directly influence our development of true obedience.

1. *Delight to do God's will.* Do you have this attitude in the inner man? God can develop it within you if you allow Him to. The following verse makes this attitude clear: "I delight to do thy will, O my God; thy law is within my heart" (Ps. 40:8).

2. *Do God's will carefully.* We must not be careless in our striving to do God's will. How careful are you in your implementing of God's will? "This day the Lord your God commands you to do these statutes and ordinances; you shall therefore be *careful* to do them with all your heart and with all your soul" (Deut. 26:16).

3. *Be sincere in your obedience.* God doesn't want only lip service, but rather He desires our sincere obedience. Strive to be honest and sincere in your obedience to God's will. "But the seed on good soil stands for those with a noble and good heart, who hear the word, retain it, and by persevering produce a crop" (Luke 8:15).

Step 4: Learn to deal with temptations. It will be important that the new Christian learn to deal with temptations to develop a successful life of obedience. Follow-up Appointment VII teaches how to react to temptation, so not much should be said at this point beyond mentioning it. Tell the new Christian you will explain this step in more detail at the next appointment.

No temptation has seized you except what is common to man. And God is faithful; he will not let you be tempted beyond what you can bear. But when you are tempted, he will also provide a way out so that you can stand up under it (1 Cor. 10:13).

It will be helpful to end this appointment by giving the new Christian some practical suggestions as to areas of his life that require obedience. The following is a helpful list to give you an idea how to communicate the practical areas for obedience:

1. Witnessing
2. Church involvement
3. Prayer
4. Bible study and devotions
5. Job
6. Mate
7. Time management
8. Priorities
9. etc.

IV. ASSIGNMENTS

A. Have him continue his notebook of devotional study.

B. Check up on his church involvement.

C. Have him continue reading previously assigned books.

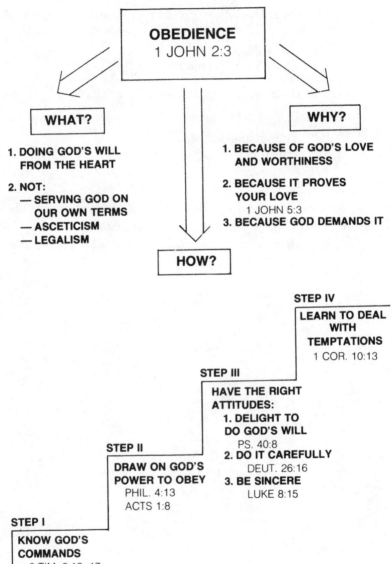

OBEDIENCE
1 JOHN 2:3

WHAT?

1. DOING GOD'S WILL
FROM THE HEART

2. NOT:
— SERVING GOD ON
OUR OWN TERMS
— ASCETICISM
— LEGALISM

WHY?

1. BECAUSE OF GOD'S LOVE
AND WORTHINESS

2. BECAUSE IT PROVES
YOUR LOVE
1 JOHN 5:3
3. BECAUSE GOD DEMANDS IT

HOW?

STEP IV
LEARN TO DEAL
WITH
TEMPTATIONS
1 COR. 10:13

STEP III
HAVE THE RIGHT
ATTITUDES:
1. DELIGHT TO
DO GOD'S WILL
PS. 40:8
2. DO IT CAREFULLY
DEUT. 26:16
3. BE SINCERE
LUKE 8:15

STEP II
DRAW ON GOD'S
POWER TO OBEY
PHIL. 4:13
ACTS 1:8

STEP I
KNOW GOD'S
COMMANDS
2 TIM. 3:16, 17

FOLLOW-UP APPOINTMENT
VII

DEALING WITH TEMPTATIONS

I. OBJECTIVES

    A. To help the new Christian understand what temptations actually are.

    B. To identify the sources of temptation.

    C. To put forth the conditions for lasting victory over temptations.

II. REVIEW

    A. Review his notebook of devotional study. Ask him to share with you new truths God has been teaching him.

    B. Review the previous lesson by asking the following questions.

        1. What does it mean to be obedient?

        2. Why should we be obedient?

        3. What are the steps to becoming consistently obedient?

        4. What are some practical areas requiring obedience in our lives?

    C. Answer any questions that he might have.

III. LESSON: DEALING WITH TEMPTATION

> No temptation has seized you except what is common to man. And God is faithful; he will not let you be tempted beyond what you can bear. But when you are tempted he will also provide a way out so that you can stand up under it (1 Cor. 10:13).

The new believer must understand how to deal with temptation if he is ever going to become a mature Christian. Temptation is the initial urging a person feels to commit sin. In itself, temptation is not sin. However, if not dealt with correctly, it can become sin rapidly. Emphasize both of these points with the new Christian. In many cases, new Christians feel that temptation is sin and that to have been tempted is to have sinned. They must be shown this is not true. Also, a new believer often takes an apathetic attitude toward temptation and the result is usually sin in his life. Be sure the new Christian clearly understands all of the points in this lesson.

SOURCES OF TEMPTATION

The Bible teaches that temptations to sin come from three sources. The following paragraphs explain each of these sources.

1. *Satan (the Devil).* Satan is clearly shown in Scripture as a source of temptation to sin. From the opening Book of Genesis to the closing Book of Revelation, we see Satan at work seeking to deceive and tempt people to sin. A new Christian is not immune to this threat. He must be made to see the tricks of Satan and realize that he will be tempted in this way. The following verses are helpful at this point: Genesis 3:1-5; 1 Peter 5:8; Revelation 20:1-3.

2. *The Flesh.* This source refers to the old sin nature within you. This old nature fights a lifelong battle with the new nature of the Christian, seeking to get the Christian to fall into old habits of life and become selfish. The new Christian must learn to expect temptations from this source and how to deal with them. The following verses identify this source: Romans 8:5-13; Galatians 5:16-26.

3. *The World.* This source of temptation involves the subtle attempts to conform a Christian to the attitudes and atmosphere of his environment. These are the temptations to look for: security in possessions or accomplishments; viewing life as livable apart from vital relationship to God; other ideas that spring from a godless and fallen society. The new Christian must be alert to these temptations and deal with them. The following verses identify this source: John 16:33; Romans 12:2; 1 Timothy 6:10; 1 John 2:15.

CONDITIONS FOR VICTORY

The Bible outlines for us the general conditions for achieving victory over temptation. The most important ones are put forth in this appointment. Explain these clearly to the new Christian.

Condition 1: Be alert. In many cases a Christian is defeated because he was not alert to the possibility of temptation. The Christian feels either of two ways: he is immune to being tempted or he can successfully fight any temptation that might come about. These are dangerous attitudes and lead to much defeat. Alert him to the sources of temptation and challenge him to be on guard against them. See 1 Corinthians 16:13; 1 Peter 5:8; Revelation 3:2.

Condition 2: Be filled. A Christian can never successfully defeat temptation in his own strength. It is only through the power of the Holy Spirit that victory becomes possible. Challenge the new Christian to be sure he is filled with the Holy Spirit. The best way for him to do this is to be sure he is meeting the conditions for filling that were outlined in Follow-up Appointment IV. Refer to Acts 1:8; Ephesians 5:18; Philippians 4:13.

Condition 3: Be quick. Temptation must be dealt with when it arises. Don't put it off. Scripture shows a definite progression of events leading from temptation to sin in James 1:14,15: ". . . but each one is tempted when, by his own evil desire, he is dragged away and enticed. Then, after desire has conceived, it gives birth to sin; and sin, when it is full-grown, gives birth to death." By being alert to the progression seen here, it is possible to prevent the temptation from turning into sin. It is important to stress the result of waiting too long. Deal with the problem as soon as possible.

Condition 4: Know biblical escapes. First Corinthians 10:13 states that with every temptation, God promises a means of escape by which we can gain victory over it. The Bible is filled with these "means of escape." For this reason a growing knowledge of God's Word will directly affect the victory we

185

achieve. Psalm 119:11 puts this truth clearly: "I have laid up thy word in my heart, that I might not sin against thee."

Two important biblical escapes are as follows:

1. Sexual temptation — flee it, run for your life, you will be unable to fight it (2 Tim. 2:22).
2. Satanic doubts — resist by relying on the Word of God (Matt. 4:1-11; James 4:7).

Help the new Christian to discover additional biblical escapes to temptation.

Condition 5: Obey by faith. In dealing with temptations, it is important to take the biblical escape route whether you feel like it or not. If you rely on feelings to motivate you to deal with temptations, you have already lost the battle. Review the need and method of obedience found in Follow-up Appointment VI. Obeying God by faith is only possible if the new Christian is developing the habit of living by faith. He must learn to do what God says regardless of how he feels (Col. 2:6).

Condition 6: Pray for victory. Prayer plays an essential role in achieving victory in the fight against succumbing to temptation. The Bible clearly commands prayer for both our personal victory and the victory of others. It might be helpful to review Follow-up Appointment V. The following Scriptures are helpful at this point:

1. Pray for your own victory: Matthew 26:41; Mark 14:38; Luke 22:40.
2. Pray for the victory of others: the example of Paul in the Epistles

IV. ASSIGNMENTS

A. Have the new Christian continue his notebook of devotional study.
B. Have him begin keeping a notebook of biblical escapes from temptation.
C. Have him continue reading assigned books.

V. Suggested Presentation of This Appointment

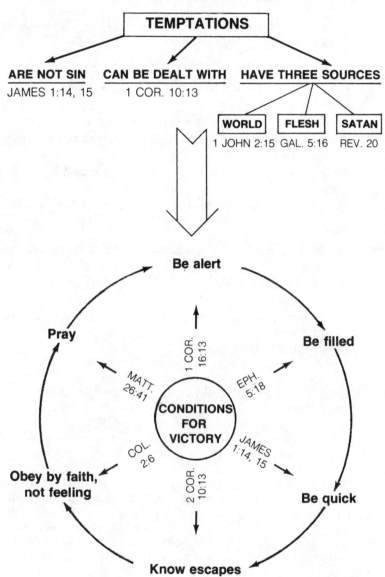

TEMPTATIONS

ARE NOT SIN
JAMES 1:14, 15

CAN BE DEALT WITH
1 COR. 10:13

HAVE THREE SOURCES

WORLD   FLESH   SATAN
1 JOHN 2:15   GAL. 5:16   REV. 20

Be alert

Be filled

Pray

CONDITIONS
FOR
VICTORY

1 COR. 16:13

MATT. 26:41

EPH. 5:18

JAMES 1:14, 15

COL. 2:6

2 COR. 10:13

Obey by faith, not feeling

Be quick

Know escapes

FOLLOW-UP APPOINTMENT
VIII

DISCERNING GOD'S GUIDANCE

I. OBJECTIVES

    A. To show that God has a wonderful plan for our lives.

    B. To show the benefits of living in the center of God's will.

    C. To show the promises of God concerning finding His will.

    D. To give some practical steps to discover God's will.

II. REVIEW

    A. Review the new Christian's notebook of devotional study.

    B. Review his notebook on dealing with various types of temptation.

    C. Review the previous lesson by asking the following questions:

        1. What is temptation?
        2. Is temptation sin?
        3. What are the sources of temptation?
        4. What are the conditions for achieving victory over temptation?

    D. Answer any other questions he might have.

III. LESSON: DISCERNING GOD'S GUIDANCE

One of the benefits of salvation is the promise of divine direction in our lives. No longer are we the victims of blind chance or dependent upon our limited resources for planning the future. We can now be assured of an abundant, purposeful life as we stay in the center of God's will. The purpose of this appointment is to get the new believer started in living in the center of God's will for his life.

A Schedule of Ten Follow-up Appointments

GOD'S OVERALL PLAN FOR OUR LIVES

For I know the plans I have for you, says the LORD, plans for *welfare* and not for evil, to give you a *future* and a *hope* (Jer. 29:11, *italics mine).*

Do not conform any longer to the pattern of this world, but be transformed by the renewing of your mind. Then you will be able to test and and approve what God's will is – his *good, pleasing* and *perfect* will (Rom. 12:2, italics mine).

These verses put forth a beautiful picture of God's will for the life of every Christian. God's plan for our life is never for evil, but rather for our welfare. We have the hope of a wonderful future as God's children, both now and eternally. The will of God for our lives is also revealed in Romans 12:2 as having three basic elements. First, it is a *good* plan. This refers back to and agrees with the teaching of Jeremiah 29:11. Secondly, it is a plan that is and will be *pleasing* to us in all its aspects. What a tremendous promise of fulfillment in life this gives us. Thirdly, it is a *perfect* plan. God's plan for our lives is the totally perfect plan for achieving the maximum of productiveness and fulfillment. Any other is second best. This plan refers not only to our careers, but also to all aspects of our lives. It is most fulfilling for the new Christian to begin discovering God's plan early in his Christian growth.

PROMISES REGARDING FINDING GOD'S WILL

The Bible gives a number of promises regarding the discerning of God's will which are helpful for the new Christian to understand. The following is a list of the most basic of these promises.

1. *God has promised that He will give us definite direction and guidance.* We need never be content with only vague generalities when seeking to determine God's will in a certain matter. The following verses clearly reveal this truth: Psalm 24:9,10; Isaiah 30:20,21.

189

2. God has promised to give us wisdom to discover His will. God is not trying to hide His will, but rather is trying to show it to us. God is more willing to let us know it than we are to discover it. Although there are certain conditions that must be true to discover God's will, we can be sure He is going to show it to us if we are faithful in seeking it. The following verses point this out: Colossians 1:9; James 1:5.

3. God has promised to be working within us to make us desire to do His will. Whenever it comes time to do God's will in a particular matter, God will have been working in our hearts to give us the desire to do it. This is taught in Philippians 2:13: ". . .for it is God who works in you to will and do what pleases him."

4. God has promised to warn us when we depart from His will. He has given us a basic warning device to act as a guard on our lives. This warning device is the peace of Christ in our hearts. When we lose our peace, we need to stop and discern if we are missing God's will. The verse that teaches this truth is Colossians 3:15: "Let the peace of Christ rule in your hearts . . . ." The word *rule* comes from a Greek word referring to the decision of a judge in an athletic event. It is the final deciding factor of knowing when we are in or out of God's will.

STEPS TO FINDING GOD'S WILL

There are a number of steps a Christian may take to discover God's guidance in a particular problem or need. Following is a list of the five most major ones:

Step 1: Present your body to the Lord as a living sacrifice (Rom. 12:1). It is important that the new Christian be sure he is filled with the Holy Spirit. This will insure his responsiveness and openness to God's will. A carnal condition in the new Christian's life will hinder God in making known His will. Review briefly the important conditions for being filled with God's Holy Spirit as they were presented in Follow-up Appointment IV, i.e., desire, surrender, obedience, confession (Acts 1:8; Eph. 5:18).

Step 2: Study God's Word. Much of God's will concerning actions and attitudes has already been revealed in the Bible. Gaining a knowledge of the basic truths of God's Word is crucial because God will never lead us contrary to His Word. The following verses point to the role of Scripture in discerning God's guidance: Joshua 1:8; Psalm 119:105.

Step 3: Be obedient to what is shown you. It is important that the new Christian become obedient to all of God's will as he understands it at the moment. This is necessary for two reasons. First, our obedience is a test of our desire to understand and follow all of God's will. We must be content and patient to act on what has been revealed to us. Secondly, God seldom shows us the end from the beginning. God only reveals as much to us as we can respond to effectively. Discovering more of God's will is dependent upon our obedience. It may help to review Follow-up Appointment VI briefly at this time, along with 1 John 3:22.

Step 4: Counsel with mature Christians. In seeking to find God's will in certain matters it is wise to consult with mature Christians who know us. Their counsel can be helpful because of their knowledge of the Word and their sensitivity to the Holy Spirit's direction. Although we must not look to them to make our decisions for us, their advice can be profitable. The following verses imply this truth: Proverbs 11:14; Acts 13:2.

Step 5: Be consistent in prayer. It is through prayer that we gain a sense of intimate communion with God and are more alert to His guidance. Prayer is the means of taking the burdens from our shoulders and placing them in the Lord's hands. As we pray, much will be shown us. We must be patient, however, and allow God to reveal His will according to His timing. It might be helpful to briefly review Follow-up Appointment V at this point, and to read Matthew 7:7,8; Philippians 4:6,7; James 1:5.

As the new Christian faithfully applies the truth of this lesson, he will discover increasingly the direction of God in his life. Challenge him to step out in faith and do what he feels God is directing him to do. Don't encourage him to wait for total assurance or peace before beginning. It is in the exercising of faith that these develop. If, after stepping out in faith, he is unable to gain peace, or the door closes on an opportunity, he can step back and seek the Lord's direction again. Remember, it is much easier to steer a moving car than one standing still. It is the same with the Christian life.

IV. ASSIGNMENTS

    A. Have him continue his notebook of devotional study.

    B. Assign one of the following books to be read:

        1. Bright, Bill. *Paul Brown Letter*. Arrowhead Springs, CA: Campus Crusade for Christ, 1963.

        2. *Essays on Guidance*. Downers Grove, IL: IVP, 1973.

        3. Little, Paul. *Affirming the Will of God*. Downers Grove, IL: IVP, 1973.

V. Suggested Presentation of This Appointment

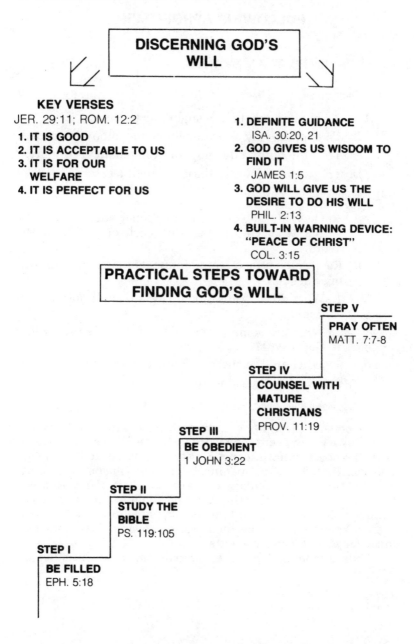

DISCERNING GOD'S WILL

KEY VERSES
JER. 29:11; ROM. 12:2

1. IT IS GOOD
2. IT IS ACCEPTABLE TO US
3. IT IS FOR OUR WELFARE
4. IT IS PERFECT FOR US

1. **DEFINITE GUIDANCE**
   ISA. 30:20, 21
2. **GOD GIVES US WISDOM TO FIND IT**
   JAMES 1:5
3. **GOD WILL GIVE US THE DESIRE TO DO HIS WILL**
   PHIL. 2:13
4. **BUILT-IN WARNING DEVICE: "PEACE OF CHRIST"**
   COL. 3:15

PRACTICAL STEPS TOWARD FINDING GOD'S WILL

STEP V
PRAY OFTEN
MATT. 7:7-8

STEP IV
COUNSEL WITH MATURE CHRISTIANS
PROV. 11:19

STEP III
BE OBEDIENT
1 JOHN 3:22

STEP II
STUDY THE BIBLE
PS. 119:105

STEP I
BE FILLED
EPH. 5:18

FOLLOW-UP APPOINTMENT
IX
DEVELOPING AN EVANGELISTIC TESTIMONY

I. OBJECTIVES

   A. To explain what an evangelistic testimony is.

   B. To explain why an evangelistic testimony is needed.

   C. To show how to develop an evangelistic testimony.

   D. To give examples of these testimonies.

II. REVIEW

   A. Review his notebook of devotional study. Share together what God is teaching each of you from His Word.

   B. Review the previous appointment by asking the following·questions:

      1. What do we know about God's overall plan for our lives?

      2. What are some promises from the Bible regarding God's will?

      3. What are the steps to finding His will?

   C. Answer any questions he might have.

III. LESSON: DEVELOPING AN EVANGELISTIC TESTIMONY

A personal testimony is an oral presentation of facts surrounding a given event. The word testimony is often associated with the courtroom. In court a testimony is not to be a clever argument or fictional happening, but rather is meant to be a clear presentation of fact. This is also true when it comes to a testimony in the spiritual realm. Your personal testimony consists simply of the facts surrounding your conversion and subsequent events. Your testimony becomes a strong evangelism tool when these facts are clearly presented.

This lesson will begin to prepare the new Christian for

sharing his faith. A prepared personal testimony is a basic tool in effective witnessing. Although it is covered in a single appointment, it might be well to spend several weeks developing this tool in the new believer's life.

WHY IS THIS TESTIMONY NEEDED?

Many Christians have never sat down and thought through the *specific* events that took place in their conversion. When confronted with the question of what receiving Christ meant in his life, the new Christian may be unable to be specific. This hurts his credibility in witnessing. When a person has spent time preparing for this question, he usually has more peace and confidence when witnessing.

Having a memorized, planned, evangelistic testimony enables the new Christian to have a ready tool for evangelism. Many situations throughout the day lend themselves to effective evangelism. There are many open doors for sharing one's testimony while in the midst of conversations with others. An added benefit of using a testimony while witnessing is the personal touch it adds to the gospel presentation. Often it is helpful to have many people sharing their testimonies in the midst of an evangelism service. This helps to show that the message does indeed change lives. It is a useful tool for the new Christian to develop.

HOW DO I DEVELOP ONE?

The following is a list of specific things to help in the preparation of an evangelistic testimony. If you have not developed yours already, do it before you seek to help the new Christian develop his.

1. Pray and ask God for wisdom and guidance as you write. God promises to give you this wisdom (review Follow-up Appointment VIII), and you can ask Him for it.

2. Develop it around a three-point outline for a clear and logical impression. Keep it relatively short (three to five minutes).

(1) Attitudes and actions before I became a Christian.
(2) Circumstances surrounding my conversion.

195

> (3) Changes that took place in my actions and attitudes after receiving Christ.

3. If you became a Christian as a child, emphasize point (3).

4. Be specific. Write at least five specific things that have occurred in each of the above categories. This might take time, but it will increase your effectiveness.

5. Give enough details to arouse interest.

6. Use some, but not too many, Scripture verses. Your purpose is to give a testimony, not to preach.

7. Edit and rewrite until it seems logical and communicates effectively.

8. Be sure to define Christian terms the non-Christian might not understand.

9. Read sample testimonies and listen to others give their testimonies to help you find ways to improve yours.

10. Memorize it.

SUMMARY

Help the new Christian get started with his testimony development. Give him yours as an example to follow. Put the new Christian in situations where he can use this tool for evangelism. It will take much work to develop an effective testimony, and the new Christian needs your encouragement and help. Review the sample testimonies that follow to gain helpful insights into the development of testimonies. Plan on this development taking several weeks.

SAMPLE TESTIMONY I

Adult

As I was growing up, I can remember attending Sunday school and church each week with my family. My relationship with God was an impersonal one, and probably the only time I really thought about Him was on Sunday. As a teen-ager I was, sometimes to my disgust, one of those "nice girls," so those years were good but uneventful.

I married a Navy ensign and it was a few years and a few

babies later before we settled in one spot for any length of time. When we did, my husband, whose Christian experience was similar to mine, and I had a real desire to become involved in a church. This we did and we became extremely busy doing church work.

About six years ago a number of events took place that greatly influenced my life. Perhaps the most significant one is that my husband received Christ into his life and became involved in evangelistic training. At first this was embarrassing to me, as I worried that people would think he was some sort of religious fanatic. However, as time went on, his enthusiasm for telling others about Christ and his spiritual growth made a deep impression on me. I saw a change in his life that I wanted to have in my own.

One morning, alone in our home, I asked Christ to come into my life as my Lord and Savior. No bells rang and I experienced no great emotional high, but I know it was the most important thing I have ever done.

Since that morning Christ has been patiently working in my life, and I praise Him and thank Him for the changes He has made. He has given me a real desire to read the Bible and to communicate with Him in prayer. He has given me the courage to knock on a stranger's door, to share Christ with that stranger. He has taken away my fear of the future. "With the LORD on my side I do not fear" (Ps. 118:6). He has shown me that nothing this world has to offer is as thrilling as to see the beautiful way He answers prayers or the way He works in people's lives, harmonizing them to His perfect will. That God whom I thought of only once a week has become the most important part of my life.

SAMPLE TESTIMONY II

Youth – Girl

As a student in junior high school, I was shy and rather unhappy with what I thought to be a dull life. I had a resentful attitude because I felt I was missing out on a lot of the fun and experiences that other kids had. My brand of Christianity made my life no better than anyone else's. In fact, because all it did was make me a good kid who went to church, I felt it was partly responsible for hindering me socially. I had grown up in the church and was truly persuaded that I was a Christian because of my church attendance and because I knew and sincerely believed certain things about God and Jesus Christ.

Doubts began to arise in my mind as to whether this knowledge really made me a Christian, however. These doubts arose when I was exposed to some people who talked about the personal relationship they had with Jesus Christ and how He had changed their lives. Not only that, but I could see something in their lives that was obviously lacking in mine. I was surprised also to hear them say they knew they had eternal life — I thought it was something you could only hope for. About this same time, members of my family started talking along this same line, and I was beginning to feel threatened by what they said. After several confrontations by them and others in evangelistic meetings, I came to understand that my head knowledge and belief about Christ were not enough. I too had to know Him in a personal way. I had to make a definite commitment to Him — ask Him to forgive my sins, be my Savior, and let Him take control of my life. At the age of fifteen I did just that and with it gained the assurance of eternal life with God that I hadn't thought possible.

I now became aware that I was truly God's child and began to experience a new hunger inside — a sincere desire to know God better — and I actively sought after this. God worked in my life in a beautiful way as I put my trust in Him, and He provided me with the fellowship and teaching I needed to grow.

Two years have gone by since I made that decision for Christ, and I can truly say they have been the best two years of my life. As time passes, Jesus Christ becomes more and more real to me; and as I see Him more, I love Him and desire to serve Him more. I still go through some times of real problems and struggles, but the victory I find as I trust in God is such that only He could provide. As I have yielded myself to Him, I have seen Him change many areas of my life. Now I look forward to the future — excited and expectant — as He reveals His plan for my life. Jesus has shown me the reality of His promise: "I have come that they might have life, and have it to the full" (John 10:10).

SAMPLE TESTIMONY III

Youth — Boy

I've been going to church every Sunday for as long as I can remember. I always listened as they talked about God, and I realized that if I was to be a Christian, it was necessary to give my life to Jesus and trust Him as my Savior. As I grew up, I knew that the other kids in school weren't Christians and I would have to be different if I was going to be one. I decided I would rather have friends. I tried to be like everyone else and did the same things they did.

I wanted my parents to think I was a Christian so they never knew about the life I lived at school and when I was with my friends. At church I put on the same "Christian" act. But all the while I knew I wasn't faking out God at all. So a painful struggle began inside of me. One part of me knew I should give my life to Christ and that I'd have to go to hell if I didn't. The other part of me said, "No, I can't! If I do, I'll lose all my friends and be lonely and miserable."

This inward conflict and my struggle with God really tormented me. So finally one night all these things came to a head. I couldn't take the hassles and the fright any longer and I gave my life to Jesus. I asked Him to forgive me for resisting Him and to come into my life as my Savior. I wanted to live my life for Him. And what a difference that simple prayer made!

No longer did I have to conform to be accepted, and I didn't lose all my friends as I thought I would. Now I could be concerned for them instead of thinking only of myself. No longer did I have to worry about faking out my family, my church, or God. No longer is there a struggle inside of me, because now I'm living for Jesus alone and life has taken on purpose. No longer am I scared of going to hell because, as God's child, I'll go to be with Him when I die.

But as I live my life from day to day, I think what means the most to me is this: Even if I had lost all my friends when I received Christ, I can honestly say it would still be worth it. You see, Jesus has become so close and true to me that I can really say, "For me to live is Christ."

The Dynamics of Personal Follow-up

IV. ASSIGNMENTS

    A. Continue notebook of devotional study.

    B. Continue to read previously assigned books.

    C. Work on evangelistic personal testimony.

V. SUGGESTED PRESENTATION OF THIS APPOINTMENT

. . . Developing your testimony . . .

I. Attitudes and actions before I became a Christian

    1.

    2.

    3.

    4.

    5.

    6.

    7.

II. Circumstances surrounding my conversion

    1.

    2.

    3.

    4.

    5.

    6.

    7.

III. Changes that took place in my life after receiving Christ — actions and attitudes

    1.

    2.

    3.

    4.

    5.

    6.

    7.

FOLLOW-UP APPOINTMENT
X
VICTORIOUS LIVING

I. OBJECTIVES

    A. To review previous truths.

    B. To systematize the elements of victorious living.

II. REVIEW

    A. Review the new Christian's notebook of devotional study. Share together what God is teaching each of you from His Word.

    B. Review the progress he has made in developing his evangelistic testimony. Offer helpful suggestions for further work.

    C. Answer any questions he may have.

III. LESSON: VICTORIOUS LIVING

This lesson, the last of the structured follow-up appointments, is not really covering anything new. The purpose is to summarize and reinforce the truths of the previous follow-up appointments. It is important that the new Christian understand how all of the truths he's been learning relate to one another. In effect, this appointment provides a checklist for effective Christian living. Develop Paul's attitude toward the repetition of your teaching: "Finally, my brothers, rejoice in the Lord! It is no trouble for me to write the same things to you again, and it is a safeguard for you" (Phil. 3:1).

CHECKLIST FOR VICTORY

1. Be sure of your standing in Christ.

Every new Christian should be certain of his standing in Christ. It will be impossible to build anything into his life if he is unsure of his salvation. The blessed assurance of eternal life and forgiveness of sin is basic to an abundant Christian life. Review if

201

necessary the points of assurance noted under Follow-up Appointment I. Emphasize the following verse:

> Examine yourselves to see whether you are in the faith; test yourselves. Do you not realize that Christ Jesus is in you — unless, of course, you fail the test? (2 Cor. 13:5).

2. Be consistent in devotions and prayer.

As has been explained before, devotions and prayer are the basic elements of developing true communication with God. It is essential that the habit of daily involvement in these actions be developed. The use of a notebook for devotions and a prayer list for effective prayer will greatly aid the development of this area of life. Review, if necessary, Follow-up Appointments II and V. Emphasize the following verses:

> Like newborn babies, crave pure spiritual milk, so that by it you may grow up in your salvation (1 Pet. 2:2).
>
> Do not be anxious about anything, but in everything, by prayer and petition, with thanksgiving, present your requests to God. And the peace of God, which transcends all understanding, will guard your hearts and your minds in Christ Jesus (Phil. 4:6,7).

3. Be consistent in fellowship.

The new Christian must understand the importance of fellowship and church involvement. An isolated Christian will usually grow cold and defeated. There is a dynamic for Christian growth found in the fellowship of Christians. Review, if necessary, the role of the church as it is put forth in Follow-up Appointment III. Emphasize the following:

> And let us consider how to spur one another on toward love and good deeds. Let us not give up meeting together, as some are in the habit of doing, but let us encourage one another — and all the more as you see the Day approaching (Heb. 10:24,25).

4. Be sure you are filled.

It is important that the new Christian be certain he is filled with God's Holy Spirit, for He is the source of all power for living and of change in our lives. Ephesians 5:18 clearly shows us that the filling of the Holy Spirit is a continuous process. The verb *be filled* really means "be ye being filled" and thus shows a continuing action. Review the conditions for filling and emphasize that we are filled by meeting the conditions for it, not merely by asking for it. The three conditions are:

    a. Desire — We must really want God to control our lives.
    b. Surrender — We must prove our desire by surrendering the control of our lives to Him.
    c. Cleansing — We must deal with any unconfessed sin as a prerequisite to being filled, because God cannot fill an unclean vessel.

Review Follow-up Appointment IV if necessary. Emphasize the following verse:

> Do not get drunk on wine, which leads to debauchery. Instead, be filled with the Spirit (Eph. 5:18).

5. *Learn to deal with temptation and sin.*

    It is necessary for the new Christian to understand that temptation is not sin, but rather the initial urging to commit sin. He should realize that God promises to give him victory over sin if he will look to Him for strength and deliverance. The new Christian should realize that temptations will come and he needs to be ready for them. The sources of temptations are the world, the flesh, and the devil. God has revealed much in His Word about how to deal with temptations, and the new Christian should be increasing in this knowledge. If he should succumb to temptation and sin, he should understand how confession works and deal with the sin immediately. Review Follow-up Appointments IV and VII for more information on these truths. Emphasize the following verses:

> No temptation has seized you except what is common to man. And God is faithful; he will not let you be tempted beyond what you can bear. But when you are

tempted, he will also provide a way out so that you can stand up under it (1 Cor. 10:13).

If we confess our sins, he is faithful and just and will forgive us our sins and purify us from all unrighteousness (1 John 1:9).

6. *Develop the habit of obedience.*

As was stressed in Follow-up Appointment VI, it is extremely important for the new believer to develop the habit of obedience. He needs the attitude of willing obedience in all that God commands and directs him to do. By being disciplined and persistent, the new Christian will succeed in following God's will as a habit of life. It is good to emphasize that this type of obedient life style is attained only when we follow God's commands, regardless of how we feel. Emphasize the following verse:

. . . and receive from him anything we ask, because we obey his commands and do what pleases him (1 John 3:22).

7. *Stay in the center of God's plan.*

It is only when a Christian is consciously living in the center of God's will for his life that he has the full and abundant life God promises to believers. God's plan for our lives is good in all respects and perfect. Review the conditions for knowing God's will as found in Follow-up Appointment VIII. Make sure the new Christian is committed to finding God's will in all aspects of his life. Emphasize the role of the peace of God in determining God's will, and point out the following verse:

Let the peace of Christ rule in your hearts . . . (Col. 3:15a).

8. *Become an effective witness.*

It is necessary for anyone who truly desires to grow in Christ to be involved in witnessing. A good way of witnessing will be the development and use of a personal evangelistic testimony. Be sure that he has been working on this tool. It would also help him to attend training conferences on evangelism and read books written on this topic. Train him personally in this area. Emphasize the following verse:

> But you will receive power when the Holy Spirit comes on you; and you will be my witnesses in Jerusalem, and in all Judea and Samaria, and to the ends of the earth (Acts 1:8).

9. Grow in your knowledge of God's Word.

Knowledge of God's Word is intimately tied into growth in Christ. Although knowledge alone will not produce growth, all the other elements of growth already noted, without knowledge, will be unable to produce true maturity. There needs to be a good balance in the new believer's life. Make sure he is getting good Bible teaching and a broad background in Christian literature. Have him begin to study Psalm 119 to gain a better perspective on the importance of the Word of God. Stress the following verse:

> All scripture is God-breathed and is useful for teaching, rebuking, correcting, and training in righteousness, so that the man of God may be thoroughly equipped for every good work (2 Tim. 3:16,17).

10. Live by faith.

Perhaps the most significant thing you can do for the new Christian is get him off the "feelings" orientation and get him on the "fact" orientation. He must learn to place his faith in what God says rather than what he feels. This is the only way he will ever become consistently obedient, consistent in devotions and prayer, and consistent in all of the other elements of effective Christian living. He must learn to trust God's Word as having the answers to his problems and obey its directions whether he feels like it or not. This is the only way his faith will survive through periods of great trials, when the external emotions are negative. This will be an emphasis that continuously needs to be made throughout your follow-up relationship with a new believer. Emphasize the following verse:

> So then, just as you received Christ Jesus as Lord, (by faith) continue to live in him (Col. 2:6).

IV. ASSIGNMENTS

A. Have him continue his notebook of devotional study.

B. Have him continue to develop his evangelistic testimony.

C. Get him into an evangelism training conference, or if none are available, train him yourself.

D. Assign the following evangelism books to be read:

1. Kennedy, D. James. *Evangelism Explosion.* Wheaton, IL: Tyndale, 1970.

2. Hendricks, Dr. Howard. *Say It With Love.* Wheaton, IL: Victor Books, 1972.

3. Little, Paul E. *How to Give Away Your Faith.* Downers Grove, IL: IVP, 1966.

4. Sanny, Lorne. *The Art of Personal Witnessing.* Chicago: Moody Press, 1957.

V. SUGGESTED PRESENTATION OF THIS APPOINTMENT

- - - - CHECKLIST FOR VICTORY - - - -

Phil. 3:1

____ **1. BE SURE YOU ARE SAVED**
2 COR. 23:5

____ **2. BE CONSISTENT IN DEVOTIONS AND PRAYER**
1 PET. 2:2
PHIL. 4:6, 7

____ **3. BE CONSISTENT IN FELLOWSHIP**
HEB. 10:24, 25

____ **4. BE SURE YOU ARE FILLED**
EPH. 5:18

____ **5. LEARN TO DEAL WITH SIN AND TEMPTATION**
1 JOHN 1:9
1 COR. 10:13

____ **6. BE OBEDIENT**
1 JOHN 3:22

____ **7. STAY IN GOD'S WILL**
COL. 3:15
ROM. 12:2

____ **8. BECOME AN EFFECTIVE WITNESS**
ACTS 1:8

____ **9. LEARN MORE OF GOD'S WORD**
PS. 119
2 TIM. 3:16, 17

____ **10. LIVE BY FAITH IN FACTS, NOT FEELINGS**
COL. 2:6

APPENDIX 2

A PERSONAL WORKER'S SUGGESTED BOOKSHELF

The purpose of this appendix is to aid the individual doing personal follow-up to develop his personal library. The books listed in this bibliography are not only for personal study, but also are excellent books to assign to a new Christian to help him in dealing with problems and assist his growth. This list reflects my personal experience with books I have found helpful and is by no means exhaustive.

CONTENTS

A. Books on Evangelism
B. Books on Follow-up and Discipleship Training
C. Books on Victorious Christian Living
D. Books on Apologetics
E. Books on Doctrine and Theology
F. Books on the Cults
G. Books on Counseling
H. Inexpensive Booklets to Give to New Christians

A. Books on Evangelism

Anderson, Ken. *A Coward's Guide to Witnessing.* Carol Stream, IL: Creation House, 1972, $3.95.

Autrey, C.E. *Basic Evangelism.* Grand Rapids: Zondervan, 1959, $1.95.

Hendricks, Howard. *Say It With Love*, Wheaton, IL: Victor, 1972, $1.95.

Kennedy, D. James. *Evangelism Explosion.* Wheaton, IL: Tyndale, 1970, $4.95.

Little, Paul E. *How to Give Away Your Faith.* Downers Grove, IL: IVP, 1966, $1.95.

Packer, J. I. *Evangelism and the Sovereignty of God.* Downers Grove, IL: IVP, 1961, $1.75.

Rinker, Rosalind. *You Can Witness With Confidence.* Grand Rapids: Zondervan, 1962, $.95.

Sanny, Lorne. *The Art of Personal Witnessing.* Chicago: Moody Press, 1957, $.75.

Spurgeon, Charles. *The Soulwinner.* Grand Rapids: Eerdmans, 1963, $2.45.

B. Books on Follow-up and Discipleship Training

Bruce, A.B. *The Training of the Twelve.* Grand Rapids: Kregel, 1971, $6.95.

Coleman, Robert. *The Master Plan of Evangelism.* Old Tappan, NJ: Revell, 1963, $1.50.

Moore, Waylon. *New Testament Follow-up.* Grand Rapids: Eerdmans, 1963, $1.95.

Trotman, Dawson. *Born to Reproduce.* Colorado Springs: Navigators, 1974, $.25.

_____. *Follow-up.* Colorado Springs: Navigators, 1974, $.25.

C. Books on Victorious Christian Living

LaHaye, Tim. *Spirit-Controlled Temperament.* Wheaton, IL: Tyndale, 1966, $1.95.

Myra, Harold. *The New You.* Grand Rapids: Zondervan, 1973, $.95.

Nee, Watchman. *The Normal Christian Life.* Fort Washington, PA: Christian Literature Crusade, 1961, $1.50.

Ridenour, Fritz. *How to Be a Christian Without Being Religious.* Glendale, CA: Regal, 1967, $1.25.

Schaeffer, Francis. *True Spirituality.* Wheaton, IL: Tyndale, 1971, $1.95.

Smith, Hannah W. *The Christian's Secret of a Happy Life.* Old Tappan, NJ: Revell, 1942, $.95.

Thomas, W. Ian. *The Saving Life of Christ.* Grand Rapids: Zondervan, 1961, $1.25.

D. Books on Apologetics

Bruce, F. F. *The New Testament Documents, Are They Reliable?* Downers, Grove, IL: IVP, 1943, $1.50.

Lewis, C.S. *Mere Christianity.* New York: MacMillan, 1960, $1.45.

Little, Paul. *Know Why You Believe.* Downers Grove, IL: IVP, 1968, $1.25.

McDowell, Josh. *Evidence That Demands a Verdict.* Arrowhead Springs, CA: Campus Crusade for Christ, 1972, $5.95.

Morison, Frank. *Who Moved the Stone?* Downers Grove, IL: IVP, 1973, $1.95.

Ramm, Bernard. *Protestant Christian Evidences.* Chicago: Moody Press, 1953, $2.95.

Schaeffer, Francis. *Escape From Reason.* Downers Grove, IL: IVP, 1968, $1.25.

————. *The God Who Is There,* Downers Grove, IL: IVP, 1968, $2.95.

Young, Edward. *Thy Word is Truth*. Grand Rapids: Eerdmans, 1957, $2.95.

E. Books on Doctrine and Theology

Berkhof, Louis. *Systematic Theology*. Grand Rapids: Eerdmans, 1946, $8.95.

Buswell, J. Oliver. *A Systematic Theology of the Christian Religion*, Vol II. Grand Rapids: Zondervan, 1972, $9.95.

Chafer, Lewis Sperry. Revised by John Walvoord. *Major Bible Themes*. Grand Rapids: Zondervan, 1974, $5.95.

Stott, John. *Basic Christianity*. Grand Rapids: Eerdmans, 1958, $1.50.

Thiessen, Henry. *Introductory Lectures in Systematic Theology*. Grand Rapids: Eerdmans, 1949, $6.50.

F. Books on Cults

Hoekema, Anthony. *The Four Major Cults*. Grand Rapids: Eerdmans, 1963, $6.95.

Martin, Walter. *The Kingdom of the Cults*. Minneapolis: Bethany Fellowship, 1968, $6.95.

Peterson, William. *Those Curious New Cults*. New Canaan, CT: Keats, 1973, $4.95.

Ridenour, Fritz. *So What's the Difference?* Glendale, CA: Regal, 1967, $1.25.

G. Books on Counseling

Adams, Jay. *The Big Umbrella*. Grand Rapids: Baker, 1972, $3.75.

————. *The Christian Counselor's Manual*. Grand Rapids: Baker, 1974, $7.95.

————. *Competent to Counsel*. Grand Rapids: Baker, 1970, $4.50.

Collins, Gary. *Effective Counseling.* Carol Stream, IL: Creation House, 1972, $2.95.

_____. *Fractured Personalities.* Carol Stream, IL: Creation House, 1972, $2.95.

_____. *Man in Motion.* Carol Stream, IL: Creation House, 1973, $2.95.

_____. *Man in Transition.* Carol Stream, IL: Creation House, 1971, $2.95.

Narramore, Clyde. *The Psychology of Counseling.* Grand Rapids: Zondervan, 1960, $6.95.

H. Inexpensive Booklets to Give to New Christians

Bright, Bill. *Transferable Concepts.* Arrowhead Springs, CA: Campus Crusade for Christ, 1971, $2.00 per set.

Brooks, Keith. *Basic Bible Study For New Christians.* Chicago: Moody Press, 1961, $.60.

Ford, Leighton. *Letters to New Christians.* Minneapolis, MN: World Wide Publications, 1967, $.35.

Munger, Robert. *My Heart: Christ's Home.* Downers Grove, IL: IVP, 1954, $.25.

Sanny, Lorne. *Lessons on Assurance.* Colorado Springs: Navigators, 1957, $.20.

Note: This is a sample of the multitude of good follow-up studies for new Christians. See your pastor, Christian Education director, or local Christian bookstore for other suggestions.